THE BIBLE TELLS ME SO

A DEVOTIONAL JOURNEY THROUGH THE OLD TESTAMENT

DR. JAZMINE ROBERTSON

Enhanced DNA Publishing
info@EnhancedDNA1.com
www.EnhancedDNAPublishing.com
317-250-5611

The Bible Tells Me So
A Devotional Journey through the Old Testament
Copyright © 2026 Dr. Jazmine Robertson
All biblical quotes are from the King James Version of the Bible.

All rights reserved.
ISBN: 978-1-967577-04-0

The Bible Tells Me So
A Devotional Journey Through the Old Testament

PREFACE

The pages of the Old Testament are filled with stories of real people—imperfect, hopeful, hurting, learning—trying to follow God just as we do today. Yet I know that, for many of us, these ancient narratives can feel overwhelming or unfamiliar. The Bible Tells Me So: A Devotional Journey Through the Old Testament grew out of my own desire to make these powerful stories feel close, accessible, and alive for anyone longing to know God more deeply.

This book is flexible by design—something you can use during quiet time alone, read alongside a friend or loved one, or explore with a small group looking for meaningful, Scripture-centered discussion. As you walk through these pages, my hope is that this devotional feels like a gentle companion—inviting you to slow down, breathe, and sit with the Word each day. Each passage, reflection, and prayer was written with you in mind, crafted to help you see God's character more clearly and recognize His faithfulness woven throughout every story. Whether you're opening the Old Testament for the very first time or returning with new questions and fresh curiosity, I pray you find comfort, clarity, and moments of connection with God along the way.

The Creation Story

Read Genesis 1:1-2:3

SUMMARY: The process of creating the earth took six days.
Day 1: God created light, separating it from darkness and establishing day and night.
Day 2: God separated the waters of the heavens from the waters of the earth and called the heavens "sky."
Day 3: God moved the water to create dry ground and called it "land," and the waters "seas." He then caused the land to produce plants and trees.
Day 4: God created lights in the sky to separate the day from the night.
Day 5: God created fish and other creatures in the water and birds in the sky.
Day 6: God created every animal on the land, including humans.
Day 7: God rested and set the seventh day apart as holy.

REFLECTION: Society often makes us feel like every moment must be spent being productive. You may have heard phrases like, "I'll rest when I'm dead," or seen people boast about always working. While there is nothing wrong with hard work, God made it a point to show us that rest has value. Rest is not something that we should feel guilty about, but instead something that we should appreciate. Without it, we risk operating out of exhaustion. We cannot help others or ourselves when we are not operating at our best.

This week, make it a priority to slow down. Take time to rest, reset, and allow God to renew both your body and your mind.

TODAY'S PRAYER: Father, thank You for the reminder to prioritize rest. Today, I surrender my anxious thoughts and my desire for constant busyness to You, and I accept Your peace. Amen.

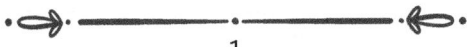

God Creates Man and Woman

Read Genesis 2:4-25

SUMMARY: God created man from the dust of the ground and breathed into him the breath of life. He placed the man in the Garden of Eden so that he could work the land and cultivate it. God formed the wild animals and birds and gave the man the task of naming each one of them. Recognizing that it was not good for the man to be alone, the Lord caused the man to fall asleep. He took one of the man's ribs and created a helper for him. The man named this helper "woman."

From the beginning of time, God had a plan for humankind. The man was given the responsibility to cultivate and supervise the garden. The woman was tasked with being his helper and partner. They were given resources and called to manage and care for what they were given.

REFLECTION: Even after the introduction of sin into the world, God's purpose for humanity has not changed. There is meaningful work to be done. God has uniquely equipped each of us with gifts, talents, and resources. Our job is to use what we have been given to glorify Him and serve others.

Have you found your purpose? Do you know what God has called you to do? Think about the gifts and talents that God has given you. Consider how you can utilize them to help others and glorify God. Most importantly, ask God for clarity. Pray that at the right time, He will reveal His purpose for your life and direct your path.

TODAY'S PRAYER: Father, I know that You have placed me on this earth for a reason. Please show me how to use my gifts and talents to serve You and bring You glory. Amen.

The First Sin

Read Genesis 3

SUMMARY: God told Adam in Genesis 2 that he could eat fruit from any tree except the tree of the knowledge of good and evil. In Genesis 3, the serpent encouraged Eve to eat the fruit from that tree, assuring her that she would not die. Eve ate the fruit and then gave some to Adam, who ate it as well. When God learned that Adam and Eve had disobeyed Him, He banished them from the Garden of Eden.

Temptation has been a struggle for human beings since the beginning of time. The serpent was able to tempt Eve by causing her to doubt what God said. That uncertainty led Eve to think that eating the fruit might be acceptable after all.

REFLECTION: Just as with Eve, the devil will attempt to twist God's Word to confuse us about what is right and what is wrong. His goal is to destroy our lives by any means necessary. However, when we are confident in what God has spoken, we are less likely to be deceived. Do not allow the tricks of the devil to destroy your life or your lineage. Spend time reading the Bible and studying Scripture so that you can hold firmly to the truth when confronted with the lies of the enemy.

TODAY'S PRAYER: Father, I thank You for providing a way of escape whenever temptation is arises. I pray that You will remind me of Your Word in moments of weakness so that I will not be deceived by the enemy. Amen.

Cain and Abel

Read Genesis 4:1-16

SUMMARY: Cain and Abel were the first two sons of Adam and Eve. As adults, Abel became a shepherd, and Cain was a farmer. When it was time to present offerings to the Lord, Cain gave some of his crops, but Abel gave the best portions from his flock. The Lord accepted Abel's offering but rejected Cain's. This rejection angered Cain, and in his jealousy, he murdered his brother. As punishment, Cain became a homeless wanderer on earth.

Cain struggled repeatedly with sin. First, he failed to give God his best. Then, he murdered his brother and attempted to cover it up. God gave Cain several opportunities to repent, but Cain continued in a cycle of wrongdoing rather than choosing repentance.

REFLECTION: Have you ever found yourself caught in a cycle of sin? Once you are in it, it can be difficult to break free. The Bible tells us that sin desires to rule over us (Genesis 4:7). When you open the door to one sin, it often leads to others. For example, telling one lie can lead to more lies in an effort to maintain it. Take heed of the warning found in the story of Cain and Abel. Repentance should always be our response to sin. Never allow yourself to reach a point where sin separates you from God's presence.

TODAY'S PRAYER: Father, thank You for being the God of restoration and second chances. I ask that You reveal any area of my life where I may be caught in a cycle of sin. Help me to release whatever is holding me back from doing what is right. Amen.

The Birth of Seth

Read Genesis 4:25-26

SUMMARY: Adam and Eve gave birth to another son. They named him Seth, for Eve said, "For God hath appointed me another seed instead of Abel, whom Cain slew."

After experiencing the trauma of losing one son at the hands of another, the birth of Seth represented a new beginning for Adam and Eve. The Bible tells us that when Seth grew up and his lineage began, people started to worship and call upon the name of the Lord. A thirst for righteousness emerged through Seth's offspring. While the legacies of Cain and Abel ended prematurely, Seth's lineage endured, producing descendants such as Noah.

REFLECTION: In this life, we will all face hardship and experience grief. While the pain may feel unbearable in the moment, it does not have to be the end of your story. God loves us and cares deeply for us. In time, He brings joy to lessen our pain. Be confident in knowing that you serve a God of restoration.

TODAY'S PRAYER: Father, I thank You that any grief or hardship that I experience will eventually be replaced with Your joy and peace. I ask that You give me strength as I await Your restoration. Amen.

The Wickedness of the Earth

Read Genesis 6

SUMMARY: The Lord saw that the people of the earth had become corrupt, and He regretted that He had created them. He decided to eliminate the human race through a flood, sparing only Noah and his family.

God instructed Noah to build a large ark so that his family and the pairs of animals could be saved. He gave Noah specific instructions for the ark and clearly told him who and what could enter it. Noah did everything exactly as the Lord had commanded him.

REFLECTION: Although the entire world had fallen into sin, God still saw righteousness in Noah and spared him and his family. Just as in Noah's time, we live in a world where sin is rampant. It may seem as if the world is enjoying life without restraint, but even in the midst of the chaos and corruption, God sees you. Do not become entangled in the temptations of the world, because judgment is coming. When you choose to live for Him, He rewards faithfulness.

TODAY'S PRAYER: Father, please help me as I face the temptations of this world. I lean on Your strength and thank You in advance for enabling me to overcome them. Amen.

Noah and the Ark

Read Genesis 7-8

SUMMARY: After Noah completed the ark, God instructed him to take seven pairs of every clean animal, seven pairs of every kind of bird, and one pair of all other animals onto the ark. Noah then entered the ark with his family.

After Noah, his family, and the animals boarded, it took an entire week before the flood started. Rain fell for forty days, and the waters covered the earth for one hundred fifty days. Scripture tells us that about ten and a half months after the flood began, the earth had nearly dried. Two months later, when it was completely dry, God allowed everyone to leave the ark.

Imagine how Noah must have felt. There was never a timeline for how long any of this would take. God gave instructions, and Noah obeyed. He did not question God during the week without rain. He did not ask how much longer when the rain continued to fall. He did not complain when it took the birds a while to confirm that the land was dry. Noah simply trusted God.

REFLECTION: Perhaps God has called you to something, but it is taking longer than expected. Let Noah's story encourage you. Do not lose hope; the rain will eventually come. Do not give up; the flooding will eventually stop. Do not get impatient; the waters will eventually recede. Keep listening, keep trusting, and keep obeying—God always keeps His promises.

TODAY'S PRAYER: Father, You know every detail of my life, including the timing. Help me to remain hopeful and positive, knowing that You are in control. Amen.

Noah's Drunkenness

Read Genesis 9:18-29

SUMMARY: After the flood, Noah planted a vineyard. One day, he drank the wine produced from his vineyard, became drunk, and lay uncovered in his tent. Noah's son Ham saw him and told his two brothers, Shem and Japheth. Shem and Japheth entered the tent, respectfully, and covered their father. When Noah later learned what happened, he cursed Ham's son, Canaan.

Noah was a righteous man, but even the righteous make mistakes. Shem and Japheth responded with dignity and respect, while Ham chose to expose his father's failure.

REFLECTION: How do you respond when friends, family, or people in your community fall into sin? Do you spread the story, or do you cover it with prayer and grace?

True Christians do not make a mockery of the downfall of others. They offer encouragement, show respect, and extend grace. They pray for their neighbors and help however they can. All of us have fallen short, and none of us would want our lowest moments to become someone else's entertainment. May we remain mindful of the grace God has shown us and extend that same grace to others.

TODAY'S PRAYER: Father, help me to respond to others with grace and compassion. Teach me to protect, not expose, and to love others as You have loved me. Amen.

The Tower of Babel

Read Genesis 11:1-9

SUMMARY: After the flood, the descendants of Noah all spoke the same language and lived in the land of Babylon. They decided to come together and build a city for themselves, along with a tower that reached the sky. When the Lord saw what they were doing, He confused the people by making them speak in different languages. Unable to understand each other, the people stopped building the city and scattered all over the world.

While unity is normally encouraged, the descendants of Noah had misguided intentions. Their unity was rooted in pride. They sought notoriety independent of God. They were so focused on self-gratification that they lost sight of God's purpose for their lives.

REFLECTION: In today's social media-driven culture, we can fall into the same trap. We live in a world where people are seeking attention and "likes" for their own gratification instead of focusing on their identity in Christ.

Our God is a jealous God, meaning that we should not put anything or anyone before Him. That includes our own plans and ambitions. God will not allow anything to prosper for long when He is excluded. The best way to avoid pride is to lean into your reliance on God. Allow His will to be the foundation of your life, and seek His guidance in all things.

TODAY'S PRAYER: Father, help me to never become so consumed with myself that I lose sight of Your purpose for my life. Amen.

Abram and Sarai in Egypt

Read Genesis 12:10-20

SUMMARY: A famine came upon the land of Canaan, so Abram and Sarai moved to Egypt. Abram feared that someone in this foreign land would kill him to have Sarai. To protect himself, he told Sarai to tell everyone that she was his sister. When Pharaoh saw Sarai, he took her into his palace. Soon after, the Lord sent plagues on Pharaoh and his household. Pharaoh discovered that Abram and Sarai were married, so he gave her back to Abram and had them escorted out of Egypt.

Abram is often remembered as a man of strong faith and obedience, but this story reveals that his faith was not without moments of weakness. Fear, driven by famine, led him to Egypt. He moved to a land where he essentially had no rights or relationships to protect him. In this foreign land, he lost sight of God's protection and provision and instead chose deception rather than trust.

REFLECTION: When faced with difficult circumstances, it can be tempting to justify sinful behavior. This mindset, however, is dangerous. Regardless of the situation, we are called to remain steadfast in doing what is right. A lack of money does not give you the right to steal, and a bad day does not excuse unkindness. Do not allow fear, hopelessness, or negativity to divert your moral compass. Choose to do what is right even when the consequences are uncertain. God will never forsake the righteous.

TODAY'S PRAYER: Father, give me the strength and wisdom to choose to do what is right at all times. Amen.

Abram and Lot Separate

Read Genesis 13

SUMMARY: Abram and his nephew Lot had both been blessed with flocks, herds, and tents, but living in close proximity led to disputes. Abram did not want the issues to affect their relationship, especially since they were family, so he suggested that they part ways. Abram allowed Lot to choose his land first, and then Abram settled in the land of Canaan.

This account of Abram and Lot provides a great example of how to successfully deal with conflict. Abram addressed the problem directly and offered a solution. He was gentle and humble in his approach, reminding Lot that family mattered more than territory. As Lot's uncle, Abram could have easily asserted authority and told Lot where to go, but he chose peace over pride and separated on good terms.

REFLECTION: Have you ever experienced a disagreement with a family member or close friend? No relationship is perfect, so misunderstandings are bound to happen. Sometimes you can quickly address problems and return to normal, but there are other instances where people are just better off apart. Separation does not mean that you don't love the person, and it does not mean that you have to be hostile towards one another. You can still support someone from afar. Be positive about the situation, stay humble, and choose peace whenever possible. After all, we are called to represent Christ in all circumstances.

TODAY'S PRAYER: Father, I pray that You give me the wisdom to handle any conflicts with respect and love. Amen.

Sarai Takes Control

Read Genesis 16:1-6

SUMMARY: Sarai was getting older in age and had not been able to bear a child. In her frustration, she had her husband, Abram, sleep with her servant, Hagar, so that she could have a child through her. When Hagar discovered that she was pregnant, she started to disrespect Sarai. In response, Sarai treated Hagar harshly to the point that Hagar ran away.

Sarai assumed that God could not use her to produce a child due to her age. By attempting to fix the situation on her own, she created turmoil within her family and added unnecessary stress to her life.

REFLECTION: At times, we can find ourselves just like Sarai, trying to fulfill God's promises based on our own timetable or expectations. Please understand that life does not work that way. God knows the future, and any delay of a promise is for a reason.

The beautiful truth of this story is that God was still able to fulfill His promise by giving Sarai a child. Yet one can only imagine how much heartache could have been avoided if Sarai had fully surrendered to Him from the beginning.

Be encouraged, God has not forgotten you. He knows the future, and He knows what is best for you. Do not lean on your own understanding. Allow Him to have full control.

TODAY'S PRAYER: Father, forgive me for ever believing that my plans for my life were better than Yours. I surrender control of my life to You. Amen.

Hagar Runs Away

Read Genesis 16:7-16

SUMMARY: The angel of the Lord found Hagar in the wilderness beside a spring of water and told her to return home and submit to Sarai's authority. The angel revealed that she would have a son named Ishmael and that her descendants would become too numerous to count. When the angel left, Hagar referred to the Lord as "Thou God seest me."

Hagar's life was likely full of moments that made her feel unseen. She had been taken away from her home in Egypt to serve in Canaan, forced to be a surrogate for Sarai, and then treated so harshly after conceiving that she ran away. Yet, in the wilderness, alone and all but forgotten, the Lord found her. He called her by her name, dealt with her gently, and promised her a mighty nation. Hagar finally felt seen.

REFLECTION: Sometimes, in the midst of obstacles, disrespect, or confusion, it can be tempting to run away from the very thing that God has created you for. You may desire to escape a season that feels unfair or overwhelming, but know that God sees you. He knows what you are going through, and He will never forsake you. The situation may not change for the better immediately, but the hardship won't last forever. Be obedient to Him and know that His promise remains the same.

TODAY'S PRAYER: Father, I thank You that no matter what I go through, You see me and You care. I ask that You give me the strength to be obedient to You through tough times. Allow me to feel Your presence and remind me of Your promises. Amen.

Abram's Name Change

Read Genesis 17

SUMMARY: God changed Abram's name to Abraham, signifying that he would become the "father of many nations." God also changed Sarai's name to Sarah to signify that she would become the "mother of many nations." The mark of this covenant was that Abraham and all his male descendants had to be circumcised. The covenant would not come through Hagar's son, Ishmael, but through Sarah's son, Isaac, who would be born the following year. That same day, Abraham took every male in his household and had them circumcised to seal his covenant with God.

At that time, Abraham only had one son by his servant Hagar. He was 99 years old, and his wife, Sarah, was 90. It certainly did not seem like the beginnings of a multitude of nations. God named Abraham not according to his current situation, but based on the future He had planned for him.

REFLECTION: God knows our name, but when we accept Christ as our savior, He gives us a new name. We all have committed sins in the past that we deserve to be labeled by, but instead God calls us holy, virtuous, and blameless. It is not that we have been so good or avoided making mistakes, but God changes our names because He sees what we will one day become through Christ's sacrifice on the cross.

TODAY'S PRAYER: Father, I thank You for looking past my present and seeing what I will become. Amen.

Sarah Laughs

Read Genesis 18:1-15

SUMMARY: One day, Abraham saw three men near his tent. He welcomed them by giving them a place to rest and having Sarah prepare food for them. One of the men told Abraham that Sarah would have a son within the next year. Sarah overheard and laughed at the thought. The Lord asked Abraham why Sarah laughed, and Sarah denied it. The Lord, however, knew the truth and said, "Nay; but thou didst laugh."

At this point, Sarah was well beyond the age of bearing children. It seemed impossible. She had likely tried to conceive many times before without success. Why would this time be any different? Most of the women her age were likely great-grandmothers, so the thought of having a child truly seemed laughable. God knew that Sarah had doubts based on her past failures and her present condition. God called out her disbelief, but He did not abandon her. He blessed her despite her lack of faith.

REFLECTION: Isn't it comforting to know that we serve a God who knows our deepest thoughts and sees all of our mistakes, but does not leave us?

Today, take time to identify an area of your life where doubt or worry has been holding you back. Pray and surrender that situation to God. Remember that God sees your heart and is faithful to act on your behalf. Choose to take a step of faith towards trusting Him.

TODAY'S PRAYER: Father, forgive me for doubting Your promises. I know that nothing is too hard for You. Amen.

Abraham Intercedes for Sodom

Read Genesis 18:16-33

SUMMARY: The Lord told Abraham that He planned to destroy Sodom due to the wickedness of the people. Abraham began interceding on behalf of the city, asking God to spare them if He could find at least fifty righteous people. He continued to negotiate with God, eventually lowering the number down to only ten, and the Lord agreed to every request.

Abraham was not perfect, but he had a strong relationship with God. Because of their closeness, God revealed His plans to Abraham. Abraham's nephew, Lot, lived in Sodom, but notice that God didn't speak with Lot. This was likely because they did not have much of a relationship. Therefore, Abraham had to intercede on behalf of his family.

REFLECTION: Do you have family or friends like Lot? Do you have loved ones who have no concern regarding their spiritual state? Allow this story to give you hope. Even though your loved one may not care to pray for themselves, God will still hear your prayer on their behalf. Continue to intercede for their protection, their guidance, and most importantly, that one day they will come to know Christ as their Savior.

TODAY'S PRAYER: Father, today I lift up my family and friends who do not yet have a relationship with You. I pray that You would open their ears to hear and soften their hearts to be receptive to You. Amen.

The Angels Protect Lot and His Family

Read Genesis 19:1-14

SUMMARY: Two angels came to Sodom, and Lot welcomed them to his home. That night, the men of Sodom demanded that Lot bring out the angels so they could sleep with them. The angels struck the men with blindness and warned Lot to get his family out of the city because Sodom was about to be destroyed.

When the angels came to survey Sodom, they witnessed firsthand the wickedness that had taken over the city. Because of God's promise to Abraham, they encouraged Lot to warn his future sons-in-law and his family to leave before the destruction. When Lot delivered the message from the angels to his sons-in-law, they did not take him seriously. They assumed that he was joking and were eventually destroyed along with everyone else in the city.

REFLECTION: When it comes to your faith, do people take you seriously? Are you living a life that makes it evident that you can hear from God? Sometimes God gives us the opportunity to deliver messages from Him to others, but if our lives are not Christ-like, how can they trust that what we are saying is true? This story serves as a wake-up call to believers. When our actions don't line up with the words we preach, it ruins our credibility. Therefore, let us be mindful to take our relationship with Christ seriously so that the world can trust us as we lead them to Him.

TODAY'S PRAYER: Father, help me to always remember that I am representing You with my words and my actions. I pray that my life will be a testimony that points others to You. Amen.

Sodom and Gomorrah are Destroyed

Read Genesis 19:15-29

SUMMARY: Lot's family hesitated to leave Sodom, so the angels led them to safety and warned them not to look back. As God destroyed Sodom and Gomorrah, Lot's wife looked back, and she was turned into a pillar of salt. Her hesitation cost her everything.

REFLECTION: Like Lot and his family, God gives us opportunities to leave toxic situations on our own. If we are slow to leave or if we refuse to leave, He may step in and force us out for our own protection.

Has God ever removed you from a bad situation—perhaps a stressful job, an unhealthy relationship, or a destructive habit? At the time, it may have felt like punishment, but in hindsight, you may recognize it as an act of mercy. Continue moving forward without looking back. Trust that God is working things out for your good. Pray that He will remove any harmful attachments that could cause you to return to your past. Be confident that anything that you lost in the previous season will be replaced with something just as good, or even better.

TODAY'S PRAYER: Father, give me the courage to release what no longer serves Your purpose in my life and the strength to obey You without hesitation. Amen.

Lot and His Daughters

Read Genesis 19:30-38

SUMMARY: After Lot and his daughters fled Sodom and Gomorrah, they settled in the mountains and lived in a cave. Believing that no men were left to carry on their family line, Lot's daughters devised a plan to preserve their father's lineage. On two consecutive nights, they got their father drunk and slept with him without his knowledge. Both daughters became pregnant by Lot. Their sons became the ancestors of the Moabites and the Ammonites.

Lot's daughters had grown up in an environment where sexual immorality was normalized. Although they moved away when God destroyed the land, the influence of that environment remained. Their actions reflected what they had been exposed to and what they believed was acceptable.

REFLECTION: It is easy to judge the daughters for their choices, but they were responding based on what they knew. Had they been taught to trust God, their response in a moment of fear and uncertainty may have been different.

This story reminds us of how imperative it is to introduce our children to God at an early age. It also serves as a warning about the consequences of exposing our children to sinful influences. As adults, we are responsible for modeling Christ for them. We must teach them that in hard times, they do not have to look to the world for answers; they can put their trust in Him.

TODAY'S PRAYER: Father, today I pray for the young people in my family and community. Guard their hearts, minds, and spirits, and protect them from influences that would lead them away from You. Cover them with Your care and order their steps. Amen.

Abraham Deceives Abimelech

Read Genesis 20

SUMMARY: Abraham and Sarah moved to Gerar, and out of fear, Abraham claimed Sarah as his sister. King Abimelech brought her into his palace, but God warned him in a dream that Sarah was married. King Abimelech returned Sarah to Abraham and gave him gifts. He allowed Abraham to choose where he wanted to live.

This story probably sounds familiar because Abraham made the same mistake in Genesis 12. By this point, Abraham should have learned to trust God to protect him in foreign lands, but this account proves that his faith was still somewhat flawed.

Though Abraham's faith wavered and he acted dishonestly, God continued to protect and provide. Even in Abraham's mistakes, God's promises remained secure, ensuring that His plan for Abraham and Sarah would succeed.

REFLECTION: Today, reflect on God's grace and mercy in spite of your sinful nature. Think about how He has protected you and your family. Consider how He has intervened and kept His promises in your life. We are so undeserving of His blessings, yet He still chooses to pour them out.

TODAY'S PRAYER: Father, thank You for intervening in my life when I was at risk of ruining Your plan. Continue to keep Your hand on my life. Amen.

Hagar and Ishmael Are Sent Away

Read Genesis 21:1-21

SUMMARY: Sarah demanded that Abraham send Hagar and Ishmael away after she caught them making fun of Isaac. Abraham was distressed by Sarah's demand, but God instructed him to do as she said. The next morning, Abraham packed food and water for Hagar and Ishmael and sent them on their way. Eventually, the water ran out, and Hagar left Ishmael to die. God heard Ishmael crying and provided them with a well full of water. He promised to make Ishmael's descendants into a great nation.

In Genesis 16, Hagar chose to obey God and return to her masters, only to later be forced to leave with nothing more than a little bit of food and water. Imagine how frustrated she must have felt being left to die. Imagine how helpless she felt having to watch her son face death. But God heard Ishmael's cry, and He provided them with what they needed in the middle of the wilderness.

REFLECTION: Have you ever reached a point of vulnerability like this? Have you ever felt like you had to watch your future, your goals, and your dreams die right before your eyes? Let this story encourage you. God hears you. He sees what you are going through, and He understands your pain. Open your eyes to God's provision in the middle of your wilderness season. Watch Him work on your behalf. Despite your current situation, God still has a plan for you. You will prosper and not fail.

TODAY'S PRAYER: Father, help me to look past the problems that I am currently facing so that I can see how You are working everything together for my good. Amen.

The Ram in the Bush

Read Genesis 22:1-19

SUMMARY: God instructed Abraham to take his son and sacrifice him as a burnt offering on a mountain. So, the next day, Abraham took Isaac and prepared to sacrifice him out of obedience to God. Abraham built the altar, but God intervened and provided a ram to sacrifice instead. God renewed His covenant with Abraham, promising him countless descendants.

Has God ever asked you to let go of something or someone that you loved? Isaac was Abraham's only son by his wife, Sarah. He was a miracle child, born to them in their old age, and the fulfillment of God's promise. Imagine how Abraham must have felt being told that he had to sacrifice what he loved most. Surely it broke his heart, but he obeyed God without hesitation.

REFLECTION: Sometimes God asks us to release the things we love to reveal whether He truly holds first place in our hearts. Know that it is only a test. If you surrender what you have, you can trust that God will restore what you gave up and may even bless you with even more.

If you're struggling with doing what God has asked of you and you are weighing the cost of your surrender, let this story encourage you to walk in obedience. Pass the test and wait in expectation as God blesses your life.

TODAY'S PRAYER: Father, I believe that it is Your desire for me to have an abundant life. Therefore, if You ask me to surrender something to You, I trust that it will lead to something better. Please give me the strength to embrace Your will even when it means surrendering my own. Amen

A Wife for Isaac

Read Genesis 24

SUMMARY: Abraham instructed his servant to find a wife for Isaac. The servant was concerned that he would not be able to find someone, so he asked God to give him a sign of confirmation. Before he had even finished praying, he encountered a young woman who was a relative of Abraham. She agreed to return with the servant and become Isaac's wife.

The servant had a difficult task. Abraham wanted the servant to go to his homeland and find a wife for Isaac so that he wouldn't have to marry a foreigner. The problem was that they lived far away. What young woman would trust a servant enough to leave her family and go all the way to Canaan, a land where she knew no one? The servant was understandably worried, but he brought his problem to God in prayer. He was specific about what he needed to see to know that he had chosen correctly, and he believed that God would honor his request.

REFLECTION: When we come to God in prayer, we must be specific about what we need. We should have faith that God can honor our requests, and we must be patient, knowing that He works according to His perfect timing. If our request aligns with God's will, we can give thanks, knowing that we will receive what we asked for. If it does not, we can still give thanks, trusting that God has something better in store for us.

TODAY'S PRAYER: Father, I know that You hear me when I pray. Help me to never withhold my requests from You. Amen.

Jacob and Esau

Read Genesis 25:19-34

SUMMARY: Jacob and Esau were the twin sons of Isaac and Rebekah. As they grew up, Esau became a hunter and outdoorsman, while Jacob preferred to stay at home. One day, Esau arrived home from the wilderness, exhausted and hungry, and found Jacob cooking stew. Jacob agreed to give Esau some of his stew, but only in exchange for Esau's rights as the firstborn son. Famished and desperate, Esau agreed and swore an oath, selling his birthright to his brother.

The danger of impatience is that it creates a false sense of urgency. Esau's desire for instant gratification caused him to focus solely on satisfying his hunger and lose sight of what it would cost him. When Esau arrived home, he did not take time to consider whether what Jacob was cooking was his best option or if there was something better available. Instead, he settled for the first thing he saw.

REFLECTION: How many of us have settled for less simply because we were impatient? Impatience pushes us to make quick decisions without consulting God and without considering the consequences of our actions. Even in moments of desperation, we should pause, assess the situation, and seek God's guidance in the decisions we make.

TODAY'S PRAYER: Father, I ask that You help me to grow in patience each day. I never want to miss out on Your best because of my inability to wait. Amen.

Isaac Deceives Abimelech

Read Genesis 26:1-11

SUMMARY: A severe famine forced Isaac and Rebekah to move to Gerar. Out of fear, Isaac lied and told the men of the land that Rebekah was his sister. Later on, however, King Abimelech saw Isaac showing affection to Rebekah and realized the truth. He confronted Isaac about the lie, but then issued a public decree warning that anyone who harmed Isaac or Rebekah would be put to death.

Like Abraham before him, Isaac prioritized his fear over his wife's safety, putting Rebekah at risk to protect himself.

REFLECTION: Scripture teaches that wives should submit to their husbands and husbands should love their wives as they love themselves. Had Abraham and Isaac done this, they would have prioritized their wives over their own fears.

For those who are married, learn from their mistakes. Actively avoid the "Gerars" in your life, the places or situations that could threaten your marriage, unless God clearly directs you there. Be intentional about protecting and prioritizing your spouse.

For those who are single, let this story guide what *not* to look for in a partner. Choose someone who values your well-being as much as their own.

TODAY'S PRAYER: Father, today I bring my relationship before You. Help my spouse (or future spouse) and me to care deeply for one another and to avoid anything that could harm the bond You have given us. Amen.

Jacob Steals Esau's Blessing

Read Genesis 27:1-28:9

SUMMARY: Rebekah overheard Isaac telling Esau that he planned to bless him. She cooked Isaac's favorite meal and had Jacob dress in Esau's clothes and cover his bare arms with hair. Jacob convinced Isaac that he was Esau and received the blessing meant for his brother. When Esau returned from hunting and discovered what had happened, he became angry and wanted to kill Jacob. Rebekah sent Jacob away to live with her brother.

Jacob and Rebekah knew that God had intended for Jacob to receive the rights of the firstborn, since Esau had already sold his birthright in Genesis 25. However, knowing that Esau was Isaac's favorite and hearing him promise to bless Esau caused fear and desperation to take over. Instead of trusting God to fulfill His promise, they decided to take matters into their own hands.

REFLECTION: How often are we like Rebekah and Jacob? God gives us a promise and confirms it, but when something threatens that promise, we stop trusting Him and try to fix the situation ourselves.

When we take matters into our own hands, we are operating outside of the will of God. While God remains faithful, our choices can still bring consequences. Let this be a warning to us to learn to trust God fully, surrender our need for control, and allow Him to work on our behalf.

TODAY'S PRAYER: Father, help me not to let my faith be shaken by what I see. Instead, help me to stand firm on Your promises. Amen.

Jacob Marries Leah & Rachel

Read Genesis 29-30

SUMMARY: Laban had two daughters: Leah, the oldest, and Rachel, the youngest, who was known to be beautiful. When Jacob arrived in Paddan-aram, he fell in love with Rachel and agreed to work for Laban for seven years to marry her. After the wedding night, however, Jacob realized that Laban had tricked him and given him Leah instead. Laban then required Jacob to work an additional seven years to marry Rachel, which Jacob willingly did. A week after Jacob married Leah, he married Rachel.

Although marrying the same man as your sister is not ideal, Jacob's effort and commitment do not go unnoticed. Even after the deception of Laban, he chose to stay and work another seven years because to him, Rachel was worth it.

REFLECTION: Let this story remind those who are single and dating to know their worth. Your love and attention are valuable and should not be given freely to those unwilling to put in the effort. Look for someone who understands your value and is willing to work to earn your heart. If effort is not given, then it may be time to move on. Jacob could have given up after he was tricked by Laban, but instead, he worked that much harder to make Rachel his wife. Life brings challenges, so seek someone who, like Jacob, is resilient enough to stay by your side and not give up.

TODAY'S PRAYER: Father, I thank You for creating me with purpose and value. Help me to know my worth and never lower it for anyone. Amen.

Leah's Desire for Love

Read Genesis 29:31-35

SUMMARY: God saw that Leah was unloved by Jacob, so He made her womb fertile while Rachel remained barren. When Leah gave birth to her first three children, she assumed that Jacob would begin to love her, but he did not. When Leah gave birth to her fourth child, she shifted her focus and gave glory to God.

God saw Leah's longing for love, and He fulfilled her need through children. While Leah acknowledged her blessings from the Lord, it is clear that initially her focus was still on what she lacked. By the time her fourth child was born, she realized, at least temporarily, that she did not need Jacob's love to fulfill her. Instead of focusing on what she lacked, she practiced gratitude.

REFLECTION: Have you ever wanted something so much that it kept you from appreciating what you had?

Sometimes God answers our prayers, but we dismiss the answer because it does not come in the way we expected. If you have been praying repeatedly for something, take a moment to inventory your life. You may find that the love, peace, or financial blessing that you have been praying for is already in front of you.

TODAY'S PRAYER: Father, forgive me for overlooking Your gifts when they do not come the way I expect. I never want to take Your generosity for granted. Amen.

Leah and Rachel

Read Genesis 30:1-24

SUMMARY: Rachel realized that she could not have children and became jealous of Leah. She had Jacob sleep with her servant so that the servant could bear children on her behalf. Later, Leah also stopped bearing children and gave her servant to Jacob. Leah accused Rachel of stealing her husband and made a deal with Rachel to get Jacob to sleep with her again. Eventually, both of the sisters had additional children of their own.

Leah and Rachel could never truly be content with their own lives because they always wanted what the other had. Leah desired the affection of Jacob, but she had the love of her children. Rachel struggled with infertility, but Jacob loved her deeply. Imagine if the sisters had simply been grateful for their own blessings and rejoiced in one another's successes.

REFLECTION: It's natural to desire improvement in our lives, but we have to stop measuring our worth based on the lives of others. When we compare ourselves to others, even a good life can feel like it's missing something. Instead, we should practice gratitude. God has given each of us our own life to live. He has uniquely gifted us and blessed us in so many ways, and if we focus on that, we can't help but be thankful.

TODAY'S PRAYER: Father, I thank You for the life that You have given me. Forgive me for the times I have envied others instead of being grateful. Help me to not allow comparison to control how I see myself. Amen.

Jacob's Wealth Increases

Read Genesis 30:25-43

SUMMARY: After fulfilling his obligation and working for fourteen years, Jacob wanted to take his family and return to his homeland. Laban asked Jacob to stay and offered him wages, but Jacob declined. Instead, he requested to keep the spotted sheep and goats and every dark-colored lamb for himself. Although Laban agreed, he deceptively removed all of the animals that he thought could produce spotted offspring in an attempt to limit Jacob's success. Despite this, God blessed Jacob to prosper, and his flocks multiplied.

From the beginning, Laban took advantage of Jacob. Not only did he reap the benefits from years of Jacob's labor, but he also benefited from Jacob's favor with the Lord. Even with all those blessings, he continued to be dishonest. While Laban meant evil towards Jacob, God turned the situation around for Jacob's good.

REFLECTION: Not everyone has good intentions towards you. Some people, like Laban, stay connected to you for the blessings attached to your life, not because they truly care for you. Thankfully, we serve a God who sees all and knows all. He knows the motives and intentions of every heart. Though others may try to take advantage of you and deceive you, their plans will not succeed. Stay close to God and continue to be obedient to His word, trusting that He will protect and prosper you.

TODAY'S PRAYER: Father, I thank You for blessing me openly, even when others are working against me. When I stay within Your will, I will always end up prospering. Amen.

Jacob Flees from Laban

Read Genesis 31

SUMMARY: Laban's sons were complaining about how Jacob had gained his wealth, and there was a change in Laban's attitude, so the Lord instructed Jacob to return to Canaan. Jacob packed and left with his family in secret. As they departed, Rachel took her father's idols. Laban caught up with Jacob a week later, scolded Jacob for leaving in secret, and accused him of stealing. Unaware of Rachel's actions, Jacob allowed Laban to search the tents. When Laban reached Rachel's tent, she deceived him by sitting on the idols. Jacob and Laban made a covenant of peace, and Laban left.

The events in Genesis 30 & 31 were all part of God's plan to lead Jacob home. First, God gave Jacob the desire to return to Canaan, and then, He made Jacob's current situation uncomfortable. Relationships shifted, tension increased, and finally, God instructed Jacob to leave. It was a challenging time, but it was necessary to usher Jacob into a new season of his life. He left without regret and with no desire to return.

REFLECTION: Often, when God is preparing us for a new season, we will notice similar patterns. Our desires may change. Things that we once enjoyed are no longer satisfying. Relationships may change, and people may treat us differently. There is no need to be afraid or second-guess yourself. This is often God at work. Draw closer to Him. Listen for His direction, be obedient to Him, and trust that everything will be okay.

TODAY'S PRAYER: Father, I thank You for the challenges that will prepare me for the next season of my life. Release me from the fear and anxiety that often come with change, and help me to surrender my concerns to You. Amen.

Jacob Wrestles with an Angel

Read Genesis 32:22-32

SUMMARY: As Jacob set up camp for the night, a man came and wrestled with him until daybreak. When the man realized that he could not overpower Jacob, he touched Jacob's hip and put it out of joint. Even though he was injured, Jacob realized that he was wrestling with an angel and refused to let go until he received a blessing. The man blessed Jacob and gave him a new name, Israel.

This account is a little unusual. A man randomly appears while Jacob is all alone, and they wrestle through the night. Who was the man? Why did he come? How did the struggle begin? Scripture gives few details, leaving more questions than answers.

REFLECTION: In life, we all experience battles that seem to come out of nowhere, whether it's a financial battle, a health battle, or even mental and emotional challenges. We may find ourselves asking, "Why is this happening?" or "How did I get here?" Jacob's story reminds us that the fight may not be easy or fair, and it may last longer than we expect. There may even be battle scars when it is over. But, at the end of Jacob's story, he walked away with a limp and a blessing. If we hold on and refuse to give up, God can bring blessing and purpose out of even our hardest battles.

TODAY'S PRAYER: Father, I ask that You give me the strength to persevere through every battle that I face. Help me to hold on to You, trusting that You will bring me through. Amen.

The Reconciliation of Jacob and Esau

Read Genesis 32:3-21 & Genesis 33

SUMMARY: As Jacob returned to his homeland, he sent messengers ahead of him to greet his brother Esau. The messengers reported back that Esau was coming to meet Jacob with four hundred men. This frightened Jacob, so he sent gifts to Esau to appease him. He divided his household into two groups so that at least one group could escape if there was an attack. When Jacob finally saw Esau, he bowed to the ground seven times before him. Esau ran to him and embraced him, and they both wept.

What a powerful story of healing and restoration. Jacob knew that even though his deception was many years ago, it was still wrong. He humbled himself and asked for forgiveness. Esau chose to extend grace, realizing that his life was still good in spite of what Jacob had done.

REFLECTION: Asking for forgiveness is not easy. It requires humility and a willingness to admit wrongdoing, with no guarantee of reconciliation. Yet repentance is essential for healing. The story of Jacob and Esau reminds us that even after long periods of separation or pain, there is still an opportunity for restoration when hearts are willing.

Is there someone from whom you need to request forgiveness? Sit with that question. Ask God to reveal where reconciliation is needed and to guide you in restoring what has been broken.

TODAY'S PRAYER: Father, I ask that You give me the courage to seek forgiveness from those I have wronged. Bring healing and restoration where it is needed. Amen.

Dinah and Shechem

Read Genesis 34

SUMMARY: Dinah, the daughter of Jacob and Leah, was raped by Shechem, a local prince. When Dinah's brothers discovered what had happened, they were enraged. They made an agreement with Shechem's father, Hamor, that Shechem could marry Dinah, but only if all the males of the city were circumcised. While the men were still recovering, Dinah's brothers attacked, killing all the men and looting everything.

Jacob and his family were living in Canaan, but they did not serve the god of Canaan. Circumcision was a sign of the covenant that God made with Abraham. Asking the Canaanites to be circumcised was troubling, as they did not understand its meaning or spiritual significance. They followed the instruction without knowing the covenant behind it, turning a sacred practice into a tool for deception and violence.

REFLECTION: At times, we as Christians can be like Jacob's family. We want the world to conform to Christian standards and principles without providing compassion or context. Do we really think that rules alone will draw unbelievers to Christ if they are not paired with His love?

Yes, it is our responsibility to share the Gospel, but let us make sure that our intentions are pure. Let us be intentional about not pushing customs without providing understanding. Let us share the entire story of Christ and not just the parts that serve an alternative motive.

TODAY'S PRAYER: Father, keep my heart pure when it comes to my relationships with unbelievers. Let Your love be seen through me. Amen.

Joseph is Sold into Slavery

Read Genesis 37

SUMMARY: Rachel's son Joseph was Jacob's favorite son. He gave Joseph a special robe, which he likely flaunted in front of his brothers. Joseph had two dreams that revealed his brothers would one day bow down before him, and he did not hesitate to share this with his family. This only fueled his brothers' jealousy. They initially considered killing him, but Judah convinced the brothers to sell him into slavery instead.

Joseph came from a family that had a lot of issues. His father fled from home after deceiving his brother. Jacob then married two sisters, creating an ongoing rivalry and tension. Now, Jacob's favoritism towards Rachel extended to Joseph, which stirred envy and resentment among the brothers.

REFLECTION: Many of us can relate to growing up in families where love feels conditional, favoritism causes tension, or betrayal runs deep. Joseph's story shows that being the product of a dysfunctional family does not disqualify you from success. Painful experiences—jealousy from siblings, unfair treatment from parents, or broken relationships—can leave scars, but they do not prevent God from working in your life. God can take the dysfunction, the hurt, and the betrayal, and use them to build character, resilience, and purpose in your life. Your beginnings—even if messy—do not limit your destiny in God.

TODAY'S PRAYER: Father, I acknowledge the brokenness in my family and the pain it has caused. Help me to trust that You are bigger than my circumstances. Heal any wounds from family trauma, and help me to walk in the purpose You have for me. Amen.

Tamar and Judah

Read Genesis 38

SUMMARY: In the middle of Joseph's story, Scripture pauses to focus on his brother, Judah. Judah had three sons. He arranged for the first son to marry a woman named Tamar, but the Lord took the life of the first son because he was wicked. Judah then told his second son, Onan, to marry Tamar. Onan was unwilling to have a child with Tamar, so the Lord took his life as well. Judah promised Tamar that she could marry the third son when he was of age, but he failed to keep his word. As a result, some years later, Tamar disguised herself to look like a prostitute and tricked her father-in-law, Judah, into impregnating her.

When Judah first heard that Tamar was pregnant after behaving like a prostitute, he was angry and demanded immediate punishment. However, after Tamar sent the incriminating evidence that he was the father, Judah's attitude changed completely. How hypocritical for Judah to condemn Tamar when he was guilty of the same sin!

REFLECTION: Have you ever been guilty of judging someone for their sin? Christ did not call us to regulate the lives of others, but rather to live a life of righteousness ourselves. Just because someone is caught in their sin doesn't make them worse than someone who seemingly gets away with sin. Let us make it a point to work on our own hearts before we attempt to crucify others.

TODAY'S PRAYER: Father, forgive me for the times that I have acted in hypocrisy. Reveal to me any areas of judgment or insincerity in my heart and help me remove them. Amen.

Joseph in Potiphar's House

Read Genesis 39:1-18

SUMMARY: After Joseph was taken to Egypt, he was purchased by an Egyptian officer named Potiphar. Joseph served him well and eventually became Potiphar's personal attendant. Scripture notes that Joseph was handsome, and he caught the eye of Potiphar's wife. After Joseph repeatedly rejected her sexual advances, she falsely accused him of rape.

Joseph is a great example of how to resist temptation. We should never allow temptation to get in the way of our responsibilities to God or our fellow man. Joseph acknowledged that sleeping with Potiphar's wife would be a sin against God, and he understood that their relationship was more important than any momentary pleasure. The temptation persisted, but Joseph did his best to avoid it, even to the point of running away.

REFLECTION: Resisting temptation requires intention. We must be willing to avoid the places, people, and things that make us vulnerable. When avoidance is not possible, we should pray and ask God for the strength to resist and discernment. Unfortunately for Joseph, despite doing the right thing, he still ended up being punished. We'll discuss later how that ultimately worked out for his benefit.

TODAY'S PRAYER: Father, I thank You for always providing me a way to escape temptation. I ask that You give me the discernment to avoid places and people who could cause me trouble. Please give me the strength to resist the desires that I am unable to avoid. Amen.

Joseph is Placed in Prison

Read Genesis 39:19-23

SUMMARY: Potiphar was upset by his wife's accusations about Joseph, so he had Joseph thrown into prison. Just as he had done in Potiphar's house, Joseph succeeded in everything he did at the prison. The Lord was with him, and before long, the warden put him in charge of the other prisoners.

Joseph now faced another undeserved setback. With one lie, Potiphar's wife sent him to prison. Joseph had dreams that his brothers would bow down to him, but now he found himself betrayed, enslaved, and imprisoned. Joseph may have felt deserted and forgotten by God, but Scripture reminds us that the Lord was with Joseph and continued to show him favor.

REFLECTION: At times, we can feel as though we are imprisoned by life. It can be tough to experience one disappointment after another and obstacle after obstacle. In those seasons, it is easy to wonder if God cares or if He has left us.

If you currently feel this way, allow this story to minister to you. God is with you even in your "prison" moments. He has not abandoned you. He sees you, He loves you, and He is still at work. Don't give up. Trust the One who holds the keys to the "prison." Soon, this season will be over, and better days will come.

TODAY'S PRAYER: Father, sometimes it's hard to understand why I have to experience tough times, but then I remember that even Jesus suffered. I thank You that You will always be with me in my difficult moments. Continue to show me favor and give me the strength to endure. Amen.

Joseph Interprets Dreams

Read Genesis 40

SUMMARY: Pharaoh's chief cupbearer and chief baker were imprisoned, and each had troubling dreams. They told Joseph about them, and he interpreted both dreams. The chief cupbearer's dream meant that in three days he would be restored to his position. Joseph asked the cupbearer to remember him and mention him to Pharaoh. The chief baker's dream meant that he would be killed in three days. Three days later, everything happened as Joseph predicted, but once restored, the cupbearer forgot about Joseph.

Interpreting the cupbearer's dream was easy because it ended well. The baker's dream interpretation, however, was harder to deliver. Nevertheless, Joseph interpreted the dream without hesitation. He did not tell the baker what he wanted to hear; he told him what God revealed.

REFLECTION: Many of us are eager to share the cupbearer's story, but hesitant to share the baker's. God's love and salvation are easy to talk about, but discussing God's judgment can be a challenge. Revealing the truth, when shared in love, gives people the opportunity to repent and turn away from their sins. As believers, we must be careful, however, not to speak out of offense or self-righteousness. We should only say what God has told us say.

TODAY'S PRAYER: Father, I enjoy sharing about Your love and forgiveness, but it can be difficult to speak against sin. I ask that You give me the boldness to speak what You have placed on my heart and help me to do so with compassion. Amen.

Pharaoh's Dreams

Read Genesis 41

SUMMARY: Two years after Joseph interpreted the dreams in prison, Pharaoh had two dreams of his own. The magicians and wise men were unable to interpret them. The chief cupbearer remembered Joseph's gift, and Pharaoh sent for him. Joseph interpreted the dreams and explained that Egypt would have seven years of prosperity followed by seven years of famine. Pharaoh placed Joseph in charge of the entire land of Egypt.

After Joseph's promotion, his name changed, he got married, and he had two sons. Joseph named his first son Manasseh and said, "For God hath made me forget all my toil, and all my father's house." He named his second son Ephraim and said, "For God hath caused me to be fruitful in the land of my affliction." God allowed Joseph to heal from his trauma first, and then he was able to be fruitful in his new season.

REFLECTION: Have you ever experienced hard times that were difficult to forget? Perhaps you endured trauma from a family member or close friend, or maybe you're carrying guilt from a mistake you made in the past. Sometimes, we struggle to bear "fruit" in our current season because we haven't let go of the hurt from the past. Ask God to reveal what you need to release and trust Him through the healing process.

TODAY'S PRAYER: Father, help me to release the pain of my past and heal what still hurts. Give me peace so that I can move forward and live fruitfully. Amen.

Joseph's Brothers Go to Egypt

Read Genesis 42

SUMMARY: Not long after the famine started, Jacob heard that there was grain in Egypt. He sent Joseph's ten older brothers there to buy food. When the brothers arrived in Egypt, they had to come to Joseph to get the grain. He recognized them, but he pretended to be a stranger. He accused them of being spies, imprisoned Simeon, and demanded that they leave and return with Benjamin, the youngest brother. Joseph had his servants fill their sacks with grain, but he secretly returned their payments. Later, when they found the money, they were afraid.

Years earlier, Joseph's brothers made a rash decision to sell him into slavery. Now, the decision haunted them. Whenever something bad happened to them, they assumed it was punishment for what they had done.

REFLECTION: Joseph's brothers remind us that sin has lasting consequences. Their story warns us of the danger of letting emotions lead instead of wisdom. In moments of heightened emotion, it's important to pause and consider the long-term cost of our choices. What feels justified in the moment can create consequences that linger for years.

When we act solely on our emotions, we risk lifelong regret. Choose wisdom over impulse, and make decisions today that will bring you peace tomorrow.

TODAY'S PRAYER: Father, when my emotions run high, slow me down and give me wisdom. Help me make choices today that I won't regret tomorrow. Amen.

Joseph's Brothers Return

Read Genesis 43

SUMMARY: Jacob reluctantly gave his blessing to allow Benjamin to travel to Egypt with his brothers. They packed double the money that was put in their sacks, along with gifts to give to Joseph. When they arrived back in Egypt, Joseph invited them into the palace to eat.

Up to this point, Scripture had not painted Judah as a man of good character. He suggested selling Joseph into slavery and dealt unfairly with his daughter-in-law, Tamar. But in Genesis 43, we begin to see a transformation. Judah convinces his father to let Benjamin go to Egypt and accepts responsibility for his brother's safety.

REFLECTION: Do you believe that people can truly change? Are you willing to trust someone who claims to have changed despite a painful past?

It can be difficult for us to trust that people have truly changed. Past wounds make us cautious, and disappointment can harden our hearts. We fear being hurt again or appearing foolish for extending grace, but this is what Christ calls us to do.

As believers, we are called to believe in Christ's power to transform lives—not just our own, but others' as well. While discernment is always necessary, Judah's story reminds us that God is patient and that when a heart is willing, real change is possible.

TODAY'S PRAYER: Father, I do believe in Your transformative power. Help me to model that belief in the way that I treat others. Amen.

Joseph's Silver Cup

Read Genesis 44

SUMMARY: Joseph had his servant fill each of his brothers' sacks with a lot of grain and the money that they had used to pay for the grain. He then had the servant place his personal silver cup in Benjamin's sack. As the brothers left Egypt, Joseph had his servant chase after them and accuse Benjamin of stealing the cup. Judah begged Joseph to allow him to be punished instead of Joseph.

Judah had made a promise to his father to take responsibility for Benjamin's well-being, and in this story, he kept his word. He offered himself up in place of Benjamin because of the love he had for his father.

REFLECTION: Did you know that Jesus was a descendant of Judah? Just like Judah, Jesus offered himself up as a sacrifice. We as people were born into sin and doomed to hell, but Jesus made a promise to his father to take responsibility for our well-being. He died on the cross, not because of any good that we had done, but because it was the will of his father.

Aren't you grateful for the humility and love that was shown on our behalf? Like our examples from today, we are called to do the same. What are some ways that you can sacrifice yourself for others?

TODAY'S PRAYER: Father, I thank You for Judah and Jesus' examples of self-sacrifice. Please show me how I can sacrifice myself for others as well. Amen.

Joseph Reveals Himself

Read Genesis 45

SUMMARY: Joseph instructed everyone to leave so that he could be alone with his brothers. He revealed his identity to them, and then he wept. Joseph instructed the brothers to go back to their father and share the news that he was alive. Joseph wanted them to bring their families to live in Egypt. When Pharaoh heard the news, he was pleased and gave them wagons and supplies for the journey. When the brothers returned home, they told their father, Jacob, the news, but he struggled to believe them.

Jacob had lived for years believing that Joseph was dead. He did not have hope in anything different, so this story sounded too good to be true. He needed evidence. Once the brothers repeated everything that Joseph said, and once Jacob saw the wagons from Egypt, he finally believed.

REFLECTION: Like Jacob, some people may struggle to believe that hope is still possible. They may not believe you when you try to tell them about Jesus or His gift of salvation. They may be skeptical of your words. It may sound too good to be true.

So, how do we help others believe? We share our evidence—not just facts, but lived experience. We point them to God's Word, and we share our testimony of what He has done in our lives.

TODAY'S PRAYER: Father, use my testimony, my obedience, and my life to draw hearts back to hope in You. Amen.

Jacob Blesses Manasseh and Ephraim

Read Genesis 48

SUMMARY: When Joseph heard that his father, Jacob, was nearing death, he went with his two sons to see him. Jacob told Joseph that he would claim Manasseh and Ephraim as his sons and that they would inherit land just like his other sons. As Jacob prepared to bless the boys, Joseph positioned them so that the oldest, Manasseh, would receive the right-hand blessing, and the youngest, Ephraim, would receive the left. Jacob intentionally crossed his hands so that Ephraim would receive the greater blessing.

Traditionally, the right-hand blessing was reserved for the oldest son, but this family had always defied tradition. Jacob's father, Isaac, was the second-born son of Abraham, and he received the greater blessing. Jacob was younger than Esau, but he received the bigger inheritance.

REFLECTION: Oftentimes with God, you don't get what you expect, and this includes His blessings. Sometimes we anticipate God's favor in one direction, and He chooses another. Maybe God did not allow you to get your dream job, but you found fulfillment in a different career. Perhaps God did not allow you to get the house you desired, but eventually you found another great place to call home. We won't always understand why God blesses certain things over others in the moment, but with time, it often becomes clear. Our job is to trust God's decision, knowing that whatever He blesses will ultimately prosper.

TODAY'S PRAYER: Father, teach me to rest in Your wisdom and trust that whatever You bless will ultimately lead me into Your purpose for my life. Amen.

Joseph Reassures his Brothers

Read Genesis 50:1-21

SUMMARY: Jacob died, and his sons honored his wishes by burying him in Canaan. Once Joseph and his brothers returned to Egypt, the brothers became fearful that Joseph would retaliate because of how they had treated him in the past. Joseph reassured them that he would not punish them. He promised to continue to take care of them and their children.

If anyone deserved to pay back evil for evil, it would be Joseph. His brothers had abandoned him, sold him into slavery, and faked his death. Joseph had suffered as a slave and then as a prisoner in Egypt because of their jealousy. Yet, the Bible tells us that when Joseph realized that his brothers were worried about retaliation, it grieved him. Joseph had already forgiven them, but it seems like the brothers had not forgiven themselves. After all those years, they were still carrying the weight of guilt and condemnation.

REFLECTION: Have you ever done something bad and repented but still dealt with the guilt and shame of the situation? The enemy wants you to believe that what you did is not worthy of forgiveness, but that is a lie. There is no sin that is too big for God to forgive. If you have repented and turned from evil, then God has set you free. Rest in the grace and forgiveness that God has generously given.

TODAY'S PRAYER: Father, I thank You for Your mercy and forgiveness. I acknowledge that I have made mistakes in the past, but I choose not to live in condemnation. I lay my guilt and shame at Your feet and embrace Your grace wholeheartedly. Amen.

Shiphrah & Puah Save the Israelites

Read Exodus 1

SUMMARY: The Israelites multiplied in number and became powerful in Egypt. Pharaoh feared that they would eventually rebel, so he enslaved them. He ordered the Hebrew midwives, Shiphrah and Puah, to kill every newborn Hebrew boy. The midwives disobeyed Pharaoh and protected the babies, and God blessed them.

Shiphrah and Puah were in a tough situation, but they chose to obey God instead of man. Their courage saved lives and allowed God's plan to continue.

REFLECTION: What do you do when your faith conflicts with the authority of the government? How do you respond when laws or mandates harm the poorest and most vulnerable people? Do you obey the law out of fear of the consequences, do you just accept that the government knows best, or do you take a stand based on your convictions?

In times when your beliefs are challenged, stand on the Word of God. Reflect on the example of Jesus and His concern for the oppressed. Continue to walk in obedience to Him, even when it isn't comfortable. Pray that God would soften the hearts of those in leadership and protect His children. Above all, have faith that God is in control.

TODAY'S PRAYER: Father, give me the strength to stand against injustice and the wisdom to know how to respond when my faith is challenged. Show me how to use my voice, influence, and gifts to help those in need and grant me peace, knowing that You are always in control. Amen.

The Birth of Moses

Read Exodus 2:1-10

SUMMARY: A man and woman from the tribe of Levi were married and had a son around the time that Pharaoh issued the order to kill all male Hebrew babies. The mother placed their baby in a basket and laid it at the bank of the Nile River. Pharaoh's daughter came to the river to bathe and saw the baby crying in the basket. She felt sorry for him and adopted him. She named him Moses.

When Moses' mother placed him in the basket by the river, she had no way of knowing that she was protecting the very one who would one day lead the Israelites out of slavery. She was just trying to keep her baby alive, but God knew Moses' future. Nothing in Moses' story happened by accident or coincidence. From the timing of Pharaoh's daughter coming to the river, to Moses' own mother being hired to nurse him, every detail was a part of God's divine plan.

REFLECTION: God has a plan for us just as He did with Moses. Whatever circumstances we find ourselves in, whether good or bad, God has already taken them into account. We can trust, obey, and worship God in the midst of any situation because we know that He is always working behind the scenes for our good.

TODAY'S PRAYER: Father, I am grateful that even when all hope seems lost, You still have a plan for my life. Amen.

Moses Murders an Egyptian

Read Exodus 2:11-15

SUMMARY: When Moses was older, he saw an Egyptian beating an Israelite. In a moment of anger, he killed the Egyptian and buried him in the sand. When Pharaoh heard what Moses had done, he tried to kill him, so Moses ran away to Midian.

REFLECTION: Have you ever witnessed someone being mistreated? Perhaps it was a waiter being scolded by an entitled customer or a child being bullied on the playground. It can be hard to watch injustice unfold and not react. Your emotions rise, and you want to come to the defense of the distressed.

The Bible encourages us not to allow anger to control us. While we should be upset when we witness mistreatment, allowing our feelings to take over can cause us to act outside of God's will. If our emotions are leading us, then we cannot be guided by the Holy Spirit.

The presence of anger should not overpower our desire to live righteously. We are still expected to respond in love. Instead of retaliating, we are encouraged to pray for those who are mistreated as well as the people who have caused harm. Allow God to bring justice in His way and His timing.

TODAY'S PRAYER: Father, it hurts me to see other people suffering, and I desire to help. I pray that You give me the wisdom to not allow my emotions to overtake me. Guide me in the way that I should help those who are mistreated. Amen

Moses and the Burning Bush

Read Exodus 3

SUMMARY: The Lord spoke to Moses from the middle of a bush that was on fire but did not burn up. The Lord told Moses that he had been chosen to lead the Israelites out of Egypt. Moses offered several excuses as to why he was not the right person for the task, but God reassured him that He would be with him.

Early in this story, we see that Moses noticed the burning bush, and when he moved closer to investigate, God called out to him. God could have spoken at any point, but He waited until Moses was attentive and focused. In verse 4, God called Moses' name twice, emphasizing that He wanted Moses to be alert and ready to listen.

REFLECTION: Have you been trying to hear from God? Are you seeking clarity or direction from Him? There are times when God wants to speak with us, but He waits until we are focused on Him and ready to listen. He doesn't want to compete with our distractions; He desires our undivided attention.

This week, take active steps to show God where your focus is. Set aside time to listen to Him. Be mindful of silencing the noise of daily life. Make it clear to God that you want to hear from Him and that you plan to be obedient to whatever He says.

TODAY'S PRAYER: Father, today I am seeking Your face. Speak to me, and I will listen. Give me direction, and I will follow. Amen.

Signs of the Lord's Power

Read Exodus 4:1-17

SUMMARY: Moses was concerned that he would not be taken seriously by the people of Egypt, so the Lord provided him with signs to help the people believe. Moses then complained that he would not be able to speak because of his speech impediment, but God assured him that He would be with him. Still, Moses begged the Lord to send someone else to Egypt. In response, the Lord agreed to allow Moses' brother Aaron to join him.

When Moses voiced his fear of not being taken seriously, the Lord instructed him to use what was in his hand. Moses threw down his staff, and it turned into a snake. God was showing Moses that he already had the tools that he needed to fulfill the calling placed on his life.

REFLECTION: Have you ever felt unprepared for something that God called you to do? If so, you are not alone. Many times God's call can seem sudden and overwhelming, but if you reflect on your past, you may notice that God has always been preparing you—equipping you with the right tools at the right time.

God frequently uses the possessions and gifts that you already have in order to execute His plan. In Moses' case, it was his staff. The message in the story is that you are enough just as you are. God simply asks for a willing heart and a surrendered life.

TODAY'S PRAYER: Father, thank You for using ordinary people like me to do extraordinary things. Amen.

The Circumcision of Gershom

Read Exodus 4:18-26

SUMMARY: As Moses was on the way to Egypt with his family, the Lord confronted Moses and almost killed him. Moses' wife quickly took a knife and circumcised their son, and God spared Moses.

Moses was an Israelite, but his wife Zipporah was a Midianite. Moses was raising their son Gershom based on Midianite customs, so Gershom had not been circumcised. This is why God confronted Moses. How could Moses instruct the Israelite people to adhere to God's laws when his own family was not following the same rules and regulations? God's message was clear: before you lead God's children, your own house must be in order.

REFLECTION: Sometimes God has a work for us to do, but He will not allow us to step fully into our calling until our lives are aligned with His will. Perhaps God wants you to teach His word, but you are not reading your Bible regularly. Maybe God wants you to mentor the youth, but your current lifestyle is not one to be followed.

Take time to reflect today. What do you sense God is calling you to do? Have you made the necessary changes in your life to walk into that calling? If not, begin thinking about how you can make sure that you are ready to fulfill God's plans for your life.

TODAY'S PRAYER: Father, I fully submit to Your will for my life. I ask that You reveal to me any changes that I need to make so that I can be prepared to serve You faithfully. Amen.

Life Gets Worse for the Israelites

Read Exodus 4:27-5:23

SUMMARY: Moses and Aaron went to Egypt and gathered the elders of Israel together. Aaron relayed everything that the Lord had told Moses, and Moses performed the signs. The people of Israel believed that God would deliver them, and they worshiped.

Then, Moses and Aaron spoke to Pharaoh. They requested that Pharaoh let the Israelites leave Egypt to have a festival in the wilderness. Pharaoh denied the request and sent an order to the Egyptian slave drivers to make the Israelites work harder. This angered the Israelites, and they blamed Moses and Aaron for their hardship.

REFLECTION: It's easy to have faith when things are going well, but what happens when things get worse? What happens when the plan that seemed perfect ends up making life harder? Do you draw closer to God, or do you become frustrated and lose faith?

Sometimes God will send us tests to see if our faith will flourish or fail. Will we move forward knowing what He promised, or will we remain in our comfort zone that is outside of His will? God wants us to choose to believe Him regardless of how the situation looks. When we choose to believe Him in difficult moments, we show that we can be trusted as good stewards in the next season.

TODAY'S PRAYER: Father, in times of trouble, help me to keep my focus on You. Please remind me of Your promise to always be there with me. Amen.

Aaron's Staff Becomes a Serpent

Read Exodus 7:1-13

SUMMARY: Moses and Aaron went before Pharaoh's court on behalf of the Israelites. Aaron threw down his staff, and it became a serpent. Pharaoh's wise men did the same, but Aaron's serpent swallowed up their serpents. Just as God had warned, Pharaoh's heart remained hardened, and he refused to free the Israelites.

A true statement was made when Aaron's serpent ate the others. It was God's way of declaring that no power and no god could stand before Him.

REFLECTION: So many times in this day and age, we give the credit for blessings and breakthroughs to everything but God. When we get a new job, we thank the friend who referred us. When we recover from illness, we credit the medicine. When we accomplish a new goal, we praise our own hard work. But how often do we pause to acknowledge our all-powerful and all-knowing God who made it possible?

God wants us to understand that He alone is supreme. Other "gods" can try to measure up to Him, but they will never compare. Let us be mindful not to place people, possessions, or achievements before Him, and let us give Him the glory He deserves.

TODAY'S PRAYER: Father, You are amazing. Forgive me for the times I have failed to give You the glory. Help me to always acknowledge You as the source of every blessing in my life. Amen.

Plague #1 - The Plague of Blood

Read Exodus 7:14- 25

SUMMARY: Pharaoh refused to free the Israelites, so God sent a plague upon the Egyptians. Aaron raised his staff over the bodies of water, and they turned into blood. Even the water that had been stored in pots and bowls turned to blood. The fish died, the river smelled, and the water was undrinkable. Pharaoh's magicians used their magic and turned water into blood as well, so Pharaoh refused to let the Israelites go.

The Nile River was Egypt's primary source of water, and the Egyptians worshiped it. It provided drinking water and irrigated the land so crops could grow. It was a part of their daily life, but with one raise of a staff, it became useless. Through this plague, God showed the Egyptians that it was He who was truly in charge of water, not the god of the Nile.

REFLECTION: Most people today do not worship bodies of water. On the contrary, we often take them for granted. With one turn of a handle, we have access to clean water. We bathe, wash our food, and clean our clothes without a second thought of how blessed we are. We pollute the water systems without a care, while people in other countries deal with water scarcity.

Today, as you wash your hands or take a sip of water, thank God for that luxury. Think about ways that you can be a good steward of the environment. It is a gift from God, and we should not take it for granted.

TODAY'S PRAYER: Father, thank You for the natural resources that You have blessed us with. Help me to take care of the environment that you created. Be with those who lack access to clean water or food, and meet their needs. Amen.

Plague #2 - The Plague of Frogs

Read Exodus 8:1-15

SUMMARY: Moses warned Pharaoh that if he refused to free the Israelites, a plague of frogs would come upon the land. Aaron raised his staff over the waters of Egypt, and frogs came up and covered the land. Pharaoh's magicians were able to do the same. This time, Pharaoh told Moses and Aaron that he would let the Israelites go if the Lord removed the frogs. Moses prayed to the Lord, and all of the frogs died. When Pharaoh saw that the plague was over, he once again refused to free the Israelites.

When reading this passage, it's easy to be shocked at how quickly Pharaoh went back on his word. While he was suffering from the plague, he acknowledged God's power and begged Moses to pray for him. As soon as the discomfort ended, however, it was business as usual.

REFLECTION: Many of us respond to God like Pharaoh—seeking Him in times of trouble but drifting once relief comes. God is gracious, compassionate, and loving towards us, but we should never take his grace for granted. Just as in any healthy relationship, our relationship with God should not be one-sided. We could never repay Him for all He has done, but we can still show our gratitude. He created us, so we should strive for righteousness. He saved us, so we should praise Him. He forgave us, so we should serve Him.

TODAY'S PRAYER: Father, I thank You for Your agape love—Your love without limits. Forgive me for the times that I have taken Your love and grace for granted. I will show my gratitude for the rest of my life. Amen.

Plague #3 - The Plague of Gnats

Read Exodus 8:16-19

SUMMARY: Aaron did as the Lord instructed and struck the ground with his staff. When he did, the dust turned into gnats that covered the land, the Egyptians, and their animals. Pharaoh's magicians were unable to replicate this act and said, "This is the finger of God." Even so, Pharaoh remained stubborn and refused to free the Israelites.

God's purpose with the plagues was so that the Egyptians would know Him, and with the plague of gnats, that message started to come through. The plague clearly demonstrated that God's power is unmatched. No matter how hard we as humans try, our work will never compare to God's.

As the story continues, we will see that the Egyptian magicians no longer even attempt to replicate the plagues. They accept defeat and surrender to the power of God.

REFLECTION: Just like with the Egyptians, as we come to know God, His power will be revealed to us. Things will occur in our lives that we can only attribute to the hand of God. Let us not be like Pharaoh and harden our hearts to Him, but let us instead allow those moments to strengthen our faith.

TODAY'S PRAYER: Father, I stand in awe of Your miraculous power. The evidence of it can be seen all around me. May every encounter with You strengthen my faith, and may my testimony strengthen the faith of those around me. Amen.

Plague #4 - The Plague of Flies

Read Exodus 8:20-32

SUMMARY: God instructed Moses to go back to Pharaoh and warn him that if he refused to let the Israelites leave, a plague of flies would come upon Egypt. This time, however, God decided to spare the region of Goshen, where the Israelites lived. The next day, the Lord did as He said, and Egypt (except for Goshen) was overrun with flies.

With the first three plagues, there appeared to be no distinction between the Egyptians and the Israelites—God's wrath affected everyone. With the fourth plague, however, there was a clear separation. By sparing Goshen in the fourth plague, God revealed His power to the Egyptians and His care and love to the Israelites.

REFLECTION: Are you in a season where you feel disappointed by God? You've prayed, read the Bible, and waited for change, but nothing seems to improve. Let this story encourage you. Even when God doesn't send your breakthrough immediately, He can still protect you in the midst of the "plague." There may still be hard times and frustration, but God will send you small reminders of His presence—moments of peace, provision, or reassurance—to remind you that He has not forgotten about you. Freedom is coming; just endure for a little longer.

TODAY'S PRAYER: Father, sometimes my faith wavers when I experience trials and tribulations. I ask that You show yourself mighty in those moments. If I have to endure the hardship, allow me to see glimpses of Your grace and feel Your nearness. Amen.

Plague #5 - The Plague Against Livestock

Read Exodus 9:1-7

SUMMARY: Moses returned to Pharaoh and warned him that the Lord would send a deadly plague upon all of the Egyptians' livestock if he refused to let the Israelites go. As with the previous plague, the Israelites' livestock would be spared. The next day, everything happened just as Moses had said. Pharaoh continued to remain stubborn and would not free the Israelites.

Later in the chapter, God explains that He could have wiped out the Egyptians immediately instead of repeatedly asking Pharaoh for their release. Instead, God chose to give Pharaoh time to see His power and make the right decision.

REFLECTION: Thankfully, God shows that same grace and compassion. As Christians, we sin and fall short, even when we know better. We deserve to be punished, but God extends grace.

Just as He did with Pharaoh, God will give us signs when we step outside of His will. You may feel uneasy about a situation or feel convicted by the Holy Spirit. You may notice that behaviors you once enjoyed no longer satisfy you. When you see the signs, take them seriously. The longer we wait to listen to God, the more disorder and confusion we invite into our lives.

TODAY'S PRAYER: Father, I acknowledge that I am not perfect. I thank You for giving me time to repent and grow. Help me to not take that time for granted. Give me the humility to respond when You correct me. Amen.

Plague #6- The Plague of Boils

Read Exodus 9:8-12

SUMMARY: The Lord instructed Moses to throw furnace dust into the air, and painful boils broke out on people and animals. Even then, Pharaoh refused to release the Israelites.

Earlier in the story, Scripture says Pharaoh hardened his own heart. After the plague of boils, it says the Lord hardened his heart. This change can be confusing. It may sound as though Pharaoh no longer had free will, but that was not the case. By this point, Pharaoh had repeatedly chosen stubbornness, and God allowed him to continue down the path he had already chosen, using it to reveal His power and glory.

REFLECTION: It is often during times of hardship that people turn to prayer, seek Scripture, and recognize their need for God. Suffering has a way of revealing our dependence on Him. God can use anything—even the actions of sinful people—to accomplish His purposes. While we may not always understand His ways, we can trust that He is never absent and never without a plan.

TODAY'S PRAYER: Father, You are a loving and just God, and sometimes I struggle to understand why You allow evil to persist. Help me to see beyond my limited perspective. Align my heart with Yours so that I can recognize Your glory even in difficult circumstances. Amen.

Plague #7 - The Plague of Hail

Read Exodus 9:13-35

SUMMARY: Moses instructed Pharaoh to shelter his livestock and servants, explaining that any living being left outside would die from hail. Moses then lifted his staff, and the Lord sent a hailstorm over Egypt. People, plants, and animals were destroyed. The only place that was spared was Goshen. Pharaoh confessed that he had sinned and begged Moses to ask the Lord to end the hailstorm. He promised to free the Israelites, but once again, after the storm stopped, he refused to keep his word.

The plague of hail was the first plague where there were conditions. God, in His mercy, provided the Egyptians with a way to avoid punishment. Those who listened to God and acted in obedience were spared from the destruction. Those who ignored God's warning faced the consequences.

REFLECTION: Have you ever reflected on a difficult situation and realized it could have been avoided if you had listened to the advice of wise counsel? Or perhaps you realized—while in the middle of a struggle—that there was a more peaceful route that you chose to ignore. Many of our hardships are intensified because we don't listen to God's instructions. God is a merciful God. While we often deserve the consequences of our actions, He is quick to give us grace. We just have to be obedient.

TODAY'S PRAYER: Father, I thank You for Your mercy and grace that protects me from the punishment that I deserve. I pray that in times of trouble, You will give me the wisdom to make sound decisions. Help me to know Your voice so that I can be obedient to You. Amen.

Plague #8 - The Plague of Locusts

Read Exodus 10:1-20

SUMMARY: Moses and Aaron went back to Pharaoh. They warned him that if he did not allow the Israelites to leave, God would bring a swarm of locusts upon Egypt. Pharaoh agreed to let the men go, but he would not allow the women and children to leave. As a result, Moses raised his staff, and the Lord caused a strong wind to bring a swarm of locusts. The locusts covered the ground and consumed the crops that had survived the hailstorm. Pharaoh called Moses and Aaron back, confessed that he had sinned, and begged Moses to ask God to remove the locusts. Once again, the Lord removed the plague, but He hardened Pharaoh's heart so that he refused to let the Israelites go.

While it was clear that the plagues revealed God's power to everyone in the moment, God explained that He also sent the plagues so that the Israelites could tell their children and grandchildren about His power.

REFLECTION: When God performs miracles and shows His power in our lives, it isn't meant to stop with us. God wants us to pass those testimonies on. As adults, we have a responsibility to make sure that the next generation knows who God is—not just through Scripture, but through lived experiences of His faithfulness. What are you doing to make sure future generations hear about what God has done?

TODAY'S PRAYER: Father, I am so grateful that I know You as my personal Savior. I don't want my knowledge of You to end with me. I ask that You help me to boldly share my testimony to those who have not yet experienced You for themselves. Amen.

Plague #9 - The Plague of Darkness

Read Exodus 10:21-29

SUMMARY: Egypt was covered with complete darkness for three days. There was light as usual, however, in Goshen. Pharaoh told Moses that all of the Israelites could leave if they left their flocks and herds in Egypt. Moses refused the offer. Pharaoh told Moses to never return.

At this point, Pharaoh had tried to compromise with Moses four times:

1. The Israelites could sacrifice to the Lord in Egypt (Plague of Flies).
2. The Israelites could leave Egypt, but could not go far (Plague of Flies).
3. Only the men could leave (Plague of Locusts).
4. All of the people could leave, but the flocks and herds had to stay (Plague of Darkness).

The final compromise seemed reasonable, but Moses knew that it didn't align with God's promise. God had told Moses that the Israelites would not leave Egypt empty-handed, so Moses was unwilling to compromise.

REFLECTION: Sometimes the devil will try to get us to compromise. "I can date a non-believer as long as I stay strong in my faith." "I can use this item that my friend stole because at least I didn't steal it." These compromises may seem small, but don't be deceived. Once we yield, the enemy often pushes for more. Therefore, let us be like Moses and stand strong in our refusal to compromise on God's promises.

TODAY'S PRAYER: Father, help me to stand strong in Your Word and Your promises despite the tricks of the enemy. Amen.

Plague #10 - Death for Egypt's Firstborn

Read Exodus 11:1-12:30

SUMMARY: Moses told Pharaoh that the Lord would cause all of the firstborn sons to die in every family in Egypt, leading the officials to beg the Israelites to leave. Once again, Pharaoh did not listen. The Lord told Moses to have each Israelite family sacrifice a young lamb or goat, eat the passover meal while dressed for travel, and place some of the blood on the sides and top of their doorframes. When the Lord passed through Egypt to execute the plague, He spared the homes marked with blood.

As with many of the plagues, the Lord made a clear distinction between the Egyptians and the Israelites. Punishment came upon the Egyptians, but the Israelites were protected through a sacrifice.

REFLECTION: Thankfully, as sons and daughters of God, we too are spared. Because of our wrongdoing, we deserve to be punished, but the Lamb of God came and sacrificed Himself on our behalf. Through His blood, we are passed over—redeemed and protected from spiritual death.

TODAY'S PRAYER: Father, I thank You for sending Your Son as the ultimate sacrifice for my sins. No greater gift could be given to me. I pray that those who do not know You as their Lord and Savior will accept You before it is too late. Amen.

The Exodus of the Israelites

Read Exodus 12:31-42

SUMMARY: After the final plague, Pharaoh finally ordered the Israelites to leave Egypt with their flocks and belongings. The Egyptians gave them whatever they requested before they departed. On that night, approximately 600,000 men, plus women and children, left Egypt after 430 years of bondage.

Unlike most escapes, the Israelites did not have to fight or sneak away. God moved on their behalf, and they walked out of Egypt victorious. The Egyptians showed the Israelites favor and provided them with clothing, silver, and gold for the journey.

REFLECTION: Sometimes the problems that we face can feel endless—illness, financial struggles, or difficult circumstances that seem impossible to overcome. But never underestimate the power of God. Deliverance is on the way. You won't have to fight or sin to be delivered, just continue to trust and obey God. Just like the Israelites, He can deliver you quickly and make you victorious.

TODAY'S PRAYER: Father, troubling times can feel overwhelming and never-ending, but I put my trust in You. Help me to remain patient and faithful as I wait on Your timing. Amen.

Parting the Red Sea

Read Exodus 14

SUMMARY: In Exodus 13, Pharaoh finally let the Israelites go, but at the beginning of Exodus 14, Pharaoh realized what he lost and decided to pursue them. As the Egyptians closed in, the Lord parted the waters of the Red Sea, allowing the Israelites to cross safely and leave Egypt behind for good.

Fear caused the Israelites to view their past through rose-colored glasses. They no longer focused on the oppression, hard labor, or unfair treatment. Instead, they began to miss their former lives. They convinced themselves that it was better to be enslaved than to be in the wilderness, headed to an unfamiliar future, even one promised by God.

REFLECTION: At times, we can find ourselves doing the same thing. We step out in faith, confident in God's direction, but once the wilderness experience becomes uncomfortable, we begin to idolize our former life. The process takes too long, the cost feels too high, the uncertainty feels overwhelming, and suddenly, we start to miss the toxic stability of our past.

If this resonates with you, learn from the Israelites. The past is behind you for a reason. Do not allow fear to take you back to the place that God has already delivered you from. God has something new for you, and it's on the other side of your "Red Sea."

TODAY'S PRAYER: Father, I thank You for saving me from my past and placing me on a new journey. I know it is not Your will for me to turn back, so I ask for strength to continue moving forward. Amen.

The Bitter Water at Marah

Read Exodus 15:22-27

SUMMARY: After Moses led the people away from the Red Sea, they traveled in the desert for three days without finding water. When they finally came upon a body of water, the water was too bitter to drink. Moses cried out to God, and the Lord showed him a piece of wood. Moses threw the wood into the water, and it became drinkable.

REFLECTION: Like the Israelites, we often step out on faith, doing what God calls us to do, only to experience disappointment along the way. Something that we expected to work out fails, or something that we expected to be easy turns out to be complicated. In those moments, how do you respond? Do you complain and question why God led you there, or do you trust that the same God who brought you to that place will also bring you through it?

The "Marah" experiences in our lives remind us that disappointment is only temporary. Bitter seasons do not last forever. When we cry out to God instead of giving in to frustration, He has the power to transform what is bitter into a blessing.

TODAY'S PRAYER: Father, I thank You that every obstacle I face is only temporary. When my faith is tested, and disappointment sets in, help me to stay the course. I will trust in You, knowing that better days are ahead. Amen.

Manna and Quail

Read Exodus 16

SUMMARY: It had been a month since the Israelites escaped, and now they missed the food that they had in Egypt. The Lord responded by providing them food from heaven—manna and quail. Each morning, the Israelites were to gather as much food as they needed for that day. On the sixth day, however, they were instructed to gather enough food for the Sabbath as well.

Some of the people did not listen and attempted to store food until the next morning. The leftover food would spoil, breed maggots, and have a terrible smell. The Israelites had to learn to get rid of their wilderness mentality and rely on God for daily provision.

REFLECTION: In a figurative sense, as Christians, we sometimes do the same. On Sunday, we come to church (or watch online) and attempt to store enough of Jesus to last us for the entire week ahead. But a few hours of prayer and praise on Sunday are not enough to carry us through everything we may face during the week. We need our daily bread—praying and reading God's Word each day so that we can be truly filled with Christ.

Take time to reflect today: Are you receiving your daily bread, or do you only spend time with God on Sundays? If you haven't been actively seeking God on a daily basis, work on ways to change that this week.

TODAY'S PRAYER: Father, help me to set aside time every day to read Your Word and speak with You. Amen.

Israel Defeats the Amalekites

Read Exodus 17:8-16

SUMMARY: The Israelites went out to fight the Amalekites while Moses, Aaron, and Hur climbed to the top of a hill. Whenever Moses held up his staff, the Israelites prevailed, but whenever he dropped the staff, they began to lose. Moses' arms became tired, so Aaron and Hur found a stone for him to sit on. They stood on each side of Moses and held up his hands until sunset. The Lord gave the Israelites the victory in that battle.

This story shows us the power of the supporting role. Aaron and Hur were humble enough to realize that God's power came through Moses lifting his hands. They did not try to raise their hands beside Moses to share in the glory—they lifted his hands.

REFLECTION: If you've been called to support a leader, do not view your role as less important. You are essential. Leaders need prayer, encouragement, and help. And if you are a leader, recognize that you are only as strong as your supporting staff. Be grateful for those who stand by you through both the good and the bad.

TODAY'S PRAYER: Father, I thank You for reminding me that every role in Your kingdom matters. Teach me to serve with humility and faithfulness, whether I am called to lead or support. Amen.

Jethro Gives Moses Advice

Read Exodus 18

SUMMARY: Moses' father-in-law came to visit him in the wilderness. He watched as Moses listened to the disputes of the people and noticed how long the people waited to be seen. Jethro felt that the system was too much of a burden for Moses and the people. He suggested that Moses select capable, honest men to serve as leaders over designated groups of people. These leaders could handle the common disputes, and Moses would be responsible for the more complicated matters. Moses listened to his father-in-law's advice and followed his instructions.

REFLECTION: Many of us are like Moses—we think that we can do it all. We know our own capabilities, so we take on a multitude of responsibilities instead of trusting others. Unfortunately, this is not a wise long-term practice. Trying to do everything leads to burnout and failure. God does not want anyone to lead alone. Even Jesus had twelve disciples.

If we want to carry out an effective long-term plan, we must first learn to seek advice from wise counsel and then learn to depend on others. There are likely plenty of people in your network who have gifts and talents and would be willing to help you if you ask. Pray that God will show you how to delegate and reveal who to trust with responsibilities.

TODAY'S PRAYER: Father, I know that it is not Your will for me to be burned out. I ask that You help me release control of some of my duties that can be delegated to others. Show me who I can trust to get the job done. Amen.

The Ten Commandments

Read Exodus 19:1-20:21

SUMMARY: After two full days of consecration, Moses led the people out to meet with God. The Israelites heard thunder and saw flashes of lightning as God spoke with Moses on Mt. Sinai and gave him the commandments for the people. The Ten Commandments are as follows:

1. You shall have no other gods before Him.
2. You must not make for yourself an idol of any kind.
3. You must not misuse the name of the Lord your God.
4. You must observe the Sabbath day by keeping it holy.
5. Honor your father and mother, as the Lord has commanded you.
6. You must not murder.
7. You must not commit adultery.
8. You must not steal.
9. You must not testify falsely against your neighbor.
10. You must not be envious of anything that belongs to your neighbor.

God provided the commandments so that the Israelites would have a set of moral guidelines to shape their faith and daily lives.

REFLECTION: Although we have been freely given salvation through Christ's sacrifice on the cross, Christians still use the Ten Commandments as guidelines for living righteously. As the scripture says, if we love God, we should keep His commandments (John 14:15).

TODAY'S PRAYER: Father, today I come before You asking for help with obedience. You have given us rules to live by, and I desire to follow them—not out of fear, but out of love. Amen.

The Golden Calf

Read Exodus 32

SUMMARY: While Moses was on the mountain talking to God, the Israelites asked Aaron to make them some gods. Aaron collected their gold rings, melted down the gold, and molded it into the shape of a calf. Then he built an altar in front of it.

The next day, the Lord saw the people celebrating and worshiping the idol, and He became angry. He wanted to destroy the Israelites, but Moses pleaded with the Lord on their behalf. When Moses saw the calf and the dancing, he became angry. He threw down the stone tablets that contained God's laws and broke them. He burned the golden calf, ground it into powder, and threw it into their drinking water.

Aaron clearly cared about the opinions of the people more than he did about being obedient to God. The idol for the people may have been the golden calf, but Aaron's idol was the approval of others.

REFLECTION: Whether we want to admit it or not, everyone enjoys encouragement from others. There is nothing wrong with feeling that way, but it becomes an issue when you place that desire for praise over your commitment to God. God is a jealous God. We should not put anyone before Him, including the approval of family and friends. Our greatest desire should be to please Him.

TODAY'S PRAYER: Lord, I desire to please You. Help me to place no one before You. Amen.

Moses Sees the Lord's Glory

Read Exodus 33

SUMMARY: After the golden calf incident, God refused to be among the Israelites as they traveled in the wilderness. Moses begged the Lord to stay with them, and eventually God granted Moses' request. Moses then asked for the Lord to reveal his presence as confirmation that He would be with the Israelites as they journeyed into the Promised Land. The Lord hid Moses in the crevice of a rock and covered Moses as He passed by, allowing Moses to only see His back.

God not only agreed to go with Moses, but He also agreed to give Moses rest. Moses was under a lot of pressure, leading a large group of people who had already shown that they were somewhat difficult and disobedient. However, with God's presence, Moses could rest because God would guide them in the right direction, supply their needs, and protect them from danger.

REFLECTION: In this life, we will all face challenges, but we must have the mindset that Moses had in recognizing that we need God's presence. If you truly trust in the God you serve, you can find rest even in the midst of trouble, because He is in control. He will send His angels before you to protect you, and He will guide you through life's journey.

TODAY'S PRAYER: Father, I am thankful for the opportunity to experience Your presence each day and for the peace that comes with trusting in You. Amen.

The Sin of Aaron's Sons

Read Leviticus 10:1-7

SUMMARY: Nadab and Abihu, the sons of Aaron, offered unauthorized fire before the Lord—something He had not commanded. As a result, fire came out from the presence of the Lord and consumed them, and they died before Him. Moses instructed Aaron and his family not to mourn, but to continue their work as priests at the Tabernacle.

As priests of Israel, Nadab and Abihu were expected to obey the laws of the Lord. Although Scripture does not record God explicitly forbidding the specific fire they offered, He had clearly given instructions for how the offering was to be made. As a result of their disobedience, they were punished by death.

REFLECTION: Sometimes Christians will try to justify their sin because it is not directly named in Scripture, but God's silence on an issue does not mean that He has blessed it. In these situations, it is important to use your discernment. What does God say about similar situations? Would you feel convicted if you proceeded with the action? Do you think that God would be pleased? Let us be mindful that we should seek God's approval in everything we do.

TODAY'S PRAYER: Father, I want to live a life that is pleasing to You. Help me to be sensitive to the convictions of the Holy Spirit. Amen.

The Complaints of Miriam and Aaron

Read Numbers 12

SUMMARY: Miriam and Aaron were Moses' siblings. They criticized Moses because they were jealous of his position over Israel. At one point, they even said, "Hath the Lord indeed spoken only by Moses? Hath He not spoken also by us?" They wanted everyone to believe that they were just as gifted as Moses. The Lord called Miriam, Aaron, and Moses to the Tabernacle and rebuked Miriam and Aaron. He punished Miriam by giving her leprosy for seven days.

REFLECTION: Have you ever felt like you were just as talented or qualified as someone else, but they were getting all of the attention? Have you ever worked with someone on a task, only for them to get all of the credit?

Everyone has been jealous at some point—whether over appearance, status, possessions, or relationships. Jealousy can cause us to fear that we don't measure up in some area of our lives. It can lead to misdirected anger towards others. The good thing is that changing our perspective can remove jealousy.

It's important that we do not exalt ourselves but instead remain humble like Moses. We should do everything with the mindset of bringing glory to God. When we focus on God's approval, the attention of others becomes far less important.

TODAY'S PRAYER: Father, thank You for Your Holy Spirit who convicts me when I have jealous thoughts. Help me to be receptive to that conviction. Amen.

The Twelve Spies

Read Numbers 13-14

SUMMARY: As the Israelites approached the Promised Land, Moses sent twelve men—one from each tribe—to scout the land. When the twelve spies returned, ten of them gave negative reports. They felt that the Canaanites were too big and strong to defeat. Two of the spies, however, believed that if God had brought them to the land, there was no reason to fear its inhabitants. They focused on how rich and wonderful the land was.

God heard the reports and punished the Israelites by making them wander in the wilderness for forty years. The ten spies with negative reports died by plague. All of the Israelites who were adults at the time were forbidden from entering the Promised Land, except the two faithful spies—Joshua and Caleb.

REFLECTION: Sometimes God has already given us the victory in a situation, but if we don't believe it in our hearts and step out on faith, we will never experience what He has promised. Fear and lack of faith can block our blessings. Choose to trust God in the midst of the wilderness. Take action in faith and reach towards your Promised Land.

TODAY'S PRAYER: Father, when I become overwhelmed with the challenges of this world, help me to focus on Your power. Fill me with Your hope and strengthen my faith so that I can trust You in spite of what my situation looks like. Amen.

Korah's Rebellion

Read Numbers 16

SUMMARY: Korah was a Levite who was upset with Moses and Aaron because Aaron was chosen to be the high priest. He, along with two men from the tribe of Reuben, led a rebellion against Moses and Aaron. As punishment, the earth opened up and swallowed those who rebelled against God.

As a Levite, Korah was already chosen to serve in the Lord's Tabernacle and minister to the people. Instead of being grateful for the responsibilities that God had given him, Korah chose to focus on what he lacked. He allowed a spirit of discontentment to draw him away from the Lord.

REFLECTION: If we are being honest, many of us have had moments of discontentment. You may complain when someone gets promoted over you at work. You may question how someone bought a house, got married, or had a baby before you. While these feelings are common, if we allow the feelings to linger, our discontentment can lead to sin.

May we learn from this story to focus on the positive things in our own lives. Each of us has been blessed with our own special gifts to be used in the Kingdom. If God wants you in a certain position, He will place you there in His perfect timing. If He does not, find contentment with where you are and strive to honor Him there.

TODAY'S PRAYER: Father, today I choose to surrender to Your will. Allow me to find joy and peace in whatever situation You bring me to. Amen.

Moses Strikes the Rock

Read Numbers 20:1-13

SUMMARY: As the Israelites were nearing the end of their time in the wilderness, they arrived at a place with no drinking water. God instructed Moses to speak to the rock so that water would flow, but Moses struck the rock twice instead. Although water came out, Moses' disobedience had consequences—God told him he would not lead the people into the Promised Land.

Previously, God had told Moses to strike a rock for water, and it worked. This time, however, God's instructions were different. By relying on what had worked before instead of listening closely, Moses failed to fully obey.

REFLECTION: When God gives us instructions, He wants us to follow them exactly. It's not acceptable to just do the parts that work for us or to rely on what we have done in the past. Moses struck the rock because it had worked before. It didn't require much faith because he had already seen it happen. Speaking to the rock was something new. It required Moses to listen closely to God, and it required a deeper level of faith.

Perhaps God wants to do something in your life that requires you to trust Him in a different way. This story should encourage you to listen carefully, be obedient, and believe that whatever God has planned will come to pass.

TODAY'S PRAYER: Father, I ask that You give me discipline as I continue to pursue obedience. Amen.

The Bronze Serpent

Read Number 21:4-9

SUMMARY: The Israelites grew impatient in the wilderness, and they began to speak out against the Lord and Moses. As punishment, the Lord sent poisonous snakes among them, and several people were bitten and died. After the people confessed their sin, Moses prayed, and God instructed him to place a bronze snake on a pole. Anyone who looked at it after being bitten was healed.

The Israelites had a complaining problem. God had delivered them out of Egypt and had promised them a land of abundance, but the journey was taking too long. He provided them with food, but they didn't like the food. Literally every one of their needs had been met, but they still found a reason to complain.

REFLECTION: How often are we like the Israelites? We complain about our jobs, but overlook the fact that they allow us to support ourselves and our families. We complain about our homes, even though they provide shelter and security. We complain about our friends and family, but if they left, we would be heartbroken. We overlook God's daily blessings and focus on minor frustrations. This story reminds us to shift our hearts from negativity to gratitude.

TODAY'S PRAYER: Father, I thank You for providing all of my needs. Forgive me for the times that I have been ungrateful. When I feel the urge to complain, remind me of how blessed I am. Amen.

Balaam and His Donkey

Read Numbers 22-24

SUMMARY: Fearing the Israelites, the king of Moab hired a man named Balaam to curse them. The Lord did not want Balaam to do this, so as Balaam and his donkey were traveling down the road, the Lord sent an angel to block their path. The donkey could see the angel and refused to move forward, so Balaam beat him. This happened three times, but the third time God allowed the donkey to speak to Balaam. Finally, Balaam saw the angel for himself. The angel allowed him to proceed, but instructed Balaam to only say what God told him to say. Instead of cursing the Israelites, Balaam blessed them.

From the beginning, God's answer to Balaam was "no." Yet when a more appealing offer was made, Balaam hoped God would change His mind.

REFLECTION: Have you ever tried to change God's mind? Perhaps God told you to stay away from a place that you enjoyed. Maybe God wanted you to leave a job you loved, or end a toxic relationship. Regardless of the situation, it can be hard to be obedient to the will of God when His will conflicts with your desires. Like Balaam, we may try to delay, compromise, or convince ourselves that we misunderstood God. But anything outside of God's will will not last or satisfy. God's path leads to blessings, even when obedience is hard.

TODAY'S PRAYER: Father, help me to trust Your will over my own. Give me the strength to surrender my desires and walk in obedience. Amen.

The Daughters of Zelophehad

Read Numbers 27:1-11

SUMMARY: The daughters of Zelophehad wanted to inherit their father's property after he died. They had no brothers, so the property would likely have gone to their uncles instead of them. They took their petition to Moses, who presented it to the Lord. In the end, not only were the daughters given the property, but a law was also set in place for similar cases in the future.

The five daughters were so brave. They knew that as women, they had little influence in a male-dominated society, but they took a risk—and it worked.

REFLECTION: So often, we discuss the importance of helping others, but it is just as important to speak up for yourself. Self-advocacy is critical. If you don't speak up for yourself, there's a possibility that no one will know that there is a problem.

Are there situations in your life where you've been too passive? Are there issues that require you to advocate for yourself? Whether it's at home, at work, or even within your church, be brave. Take the risk, and speak up. Your words may help others just as much as it helps you.

TODAY'S PRAYER: Father, give me the wisdom to know when to speak up for myself and the courage to do so. Amen.

Moses Views the Promised Land

Read Deuteronomy 3:23-39

SUMMARY: Moses asked the Lord if he could cross the Jordan and enter the Promised Land with the new generation of Israelites, but the Lord would not allow it. Instead, He told Moses that he could view the land from afar. Then He instructed Moses to prepare Joshua to lead the people across the Jordan River.

REFLECTION: Have you ever had a season of your life come to an end? Perhaps you left a job after working for several years, or maybe you had to leave a ministry you poured your heart into. It can be hard to give up something that you've invested time, energy, and resources into, especially when you had plans and goals for the future.

God may call us to move on, not for our own sake, but for the greater purpose of His plan. Before moving on, however, we must train up the next generation so that they can excel. We must share our knowledge and wisdom with them so that our absence isn't felt. We must be transparent about our mistakes so that they don't repeat them. We must have faith that even if God doesn't allow us to experience the fruits of our labor, He will still allow us to have our "Pisgah Peak" moment and, in some way, see the fulfillment of His promises.

TODAY'S PRAYER: Father, please help me to let go of places and roles where my season has ended. Give me the grace to move forward and to invest in those who are following behind me. Amen.

The Death of Moses

Read Deuteronomy 34

SUMMARY: Moses had the opportunity to view the Promised Land before he died in Moab. After his death, the Israelites mourned for thirty days, and then Joshua assumed leadership.

Moses and the Israelites had gone through a lot together. Moses had led them out of Egypt, guided them through the wilderness, and prayed to God on their behalf. Needless to say, his death was significant, and the Israelites' thirty-day period of mourning reflected the depth of their loss. God allowed them the time to grieve, process their new reality, and prepare to move forward under Joshua's leadership.

REFLECTION: Loss—whether a person, a season, or something meaningful—is never easy. You're processing the fact that life will never be the same. You're balancing the act of reflecting on the past while living in the present.

We can learn a lot from the way that the Israelites handled grief. Their story shows us that it's okay to pause from the busyness of daily life to mourn what you have lost. You don't always have to be strong. The work will still be there when you are ready. God wants you to heal and restore your strength for the next chapter of your life.

TODAY'S PRAYER: Father, I recognize that my mourning is my way of expressing how much I cherished what I lost. Heal my heart today, and remind me of Your promise of joy in the morning. Amen.

The Story of Rahab

Read Joshua 2

SUMMARY: Joshua secretly sent two spies to scout out the land of Jericho, but somehow the king of Jericho found out. Rahab was a Canaanite woman who lived in the city. She hid the Israelite spies on her roof. In return, the Israelites spared Rahab and her family when they captured the city.

By now, you've probably noticed that God uses the most unlikely people to accomplish His will. Moses was a murderer, Jacob was deceptive, and Rahab was a prostitute. While the people of Jericho likely shunned her, it was Rahab's heart that allowed her to be used by God. She demonstrated strong faith when she said, "I know that the Lord hath given you this land." Rahab had not seen God's miracles first-hand, but based on what she had heard, she trusted that God was real. Because of Rahab's bravery and faith, her family was spared, and she ended up marrying an Israelite, becoming part of the lineage of Jesus.

REFLECTION: Perhaps you are carrying the guilt of mistakes that you made in the past, or maybe you feel that God can't use you because of your reputation. Let Rahab's story encourage you. God is not focused on who you used to be; He is looking at your heart today. When you choose to trust God and walk in obedience, transformation is possible.

TODAY'S PRAYER: Father, I thank You that regardless of what I have done in the past, there is still hope for a bright future. I receive Your transforming power today. Amen.

The Memorial Stones

Read Joshua 4

SUMMARY: After the Israelites crossed the Jordan River, the Lord told Joshua to choose twelve men—one from each tribe—to take twelve stones from the middle of the river. They carried the stones to their campsite near Jericho and stacked them there.

Joshua explained to the Israelites that the stones were meant to serve as a memorial. The future generations would not have that same experience of crossing into the Promised Land, so the stones could be used to share the story with them and make them aware of God's power and faithfulness.

REFLECTION: While we may not have twelve physical stones, we all have memories of God's faithfulness to us. That way, when trials and tribulations come into our lives, we can recall how the Lord protected us and have confidence that He can do it again. The memories that we have are not just for us. The memories should be shared with others. They are meant to be shared with our family, our friends, and even strangers, so that others can be encouraged and come to know God's goodness.

Consider this: Is there someone in your life who needs to hear about what God has done for you? Is there someone who could be strengthened by your testimony? Take time to reflect on God's faithfulness and share the Good News today.

TODAY'S PRAYER: Father, my memories of Your goodness give me hope for the future. Thank You for Your faithfulness. Amen.

The Battle of Jericho

Read Joshua 6

SUMMARY: God instructed Joshua and his men to march around the town of Jericho once a day for six days. On the seventh day, they were to march around the town seven times with the priests blowing horns and the people shouting. When they obeyed, the walls of Jericho collapsed. The Israelites charged into the town and captured it.

The Israelites wandered in the wilderness for forty years, anticipating the time when they would get to the Promised Land. Even when they were right at the gate of the Promised Land, they still had to wait for six days. The Israelites grumbled and complained along the journey, struggling with doubt and impatience. Despite their imperfections, God kept His promise.

REFLECTION: Maybe you're waiting on God to fulfill a promise in your own life. The waiting may feel long, frustrating, or even discouraging. You may wonder why, after coming so far, you still haven't seen the breakthrough you've been praying for. Jericho reminds us that even when the promise is within reach, obedience and patience are still required.

God's instructions may not always make sense to us, but His ways are intentional. Our responsibility is not to rush the process or question His timing, but to remain faithful and obedient while we wait.

TODAY'S PRAYER: Father, I am grateful that You answer my prayers in Your perfect timing. I ask that You renew my hope as I continue to wait on Your promises to be fulfilled. Amen.

Achan's Sin

Read Joshua 7

SUMMARY: Joshua sent 3,000 warriors to attack the town of Ai, but they were defeated. Joshua could not understand why the Lord would allow them to lose after He had just brought them into the Promised Land. The Lord explained that the Israelites had disobeyed Him and stolen what had been set apart as holy.

The next morning, Joshua gathered all the people. The Lord identified Achan as the one who had sinned. Achan and his family were stoned, and their bodies were burned. Then, the Lord's anger subsided.

REFLECTION: Sometimes, when we are tempted to sin, we weigh the risks and rewards as if the consequences stop with us. But Scripture reminds us that our actions often ripple far beyond our own lives. Our choices often affect our families, our friends, and even our communities.

The next time you are tempted to sin, pause and consider the people connected to you. Could your actions cause them pain, disappointment, or loss? Sometimes, remembering who we could hurt is enough to help us choose what is right.

TODAY'S PRAYER: Father, as I reflect on the past, I can acknowledge that my sins have sometimes affected innocent people. I ask that You heal any hurts and restore any losses due to my mistakes. Help me to walk in wisdom and obedience moving forward. Amen.

The Deception of the Gibeonites

Read Joshua 9

SUMMARY: The people of Gibeon heard how Joshua and the Israelites had conquered Jericho and Ai, so they pretended to be foreigners and made a peace treaty with the Israelites. Three days later, the Israelites found out that they had been tricked by the people of Gibeon. The Israelites were angry, but they could not kill the Gibeonites because of their treaty.

The Lord had instructed the Israelites to destroy any neighboring nations, but they were allowed to make peace treaties with the distant ones. The people of Gibeon were aware of this, so they approached the Israelites pretending to be from a faraway land. The Israelites were right to be skeptical, but they made the mistake of not consulting God in the process.

REFLECTION: Just like the Gibeonites, the devil doesn't always attack us head-on. Sometimes he will choose to simply deceive us. He knows the instructions that God has given us in the Bible. He knows that God has plans for us to prosper. He knows that if he is able to trick us into sin or poor decisions, it can negatively affect our relationship with the Lord, which is exactly what he wants.

The best way to avoid being deceived is to use discernment. Pray about the decisions you face. Ask the Holy Spirit to guide your steps, and then listen for His direction. It is not God's will for us to be deceived, so if we seek Him first, He will answer.

TODAY'S PRAYER: Father, I ask that You give me wisdom and discernment so that I will not be moved by the tricks of the enemy. Amen.

The Sun Stands Still

Read Joshua 10:1-15

SUMMARY: Word had spread about the Israelites' success in war, and the surrounding nations became afraid. As a result, several of them banded together and attacked the Israelites' ally Gibeon. The people of Gibeon requested help from Joshua and the Israelites, so the Israelite army came to their rescue. The Lord was with the Israelites as they attacked the Amorites. On the final day, however, Joshua needed more daylight in order to defeat the Amorites, so he prayed for the sun to stand still in the sky and for the moon to stay in place. God granted his request.

Asking God to pause the solar system would seem like an outrageous request to most of us. But, is it possible that it seems like too big a request because our faith is too small? The truth is that a limited prayer life leads to limited miracles. Sometimes we have to stretch our faith and boldly ask God for what seems to be impossible. God honored Joshua's prayer because Joshua's faith was just as big as his ask.

REFLECTION: As you reflect today, is there something impossible that you would like God to do in your life? Is there a situation that seems too big, too complicated, or too far gone? Let this story encourage you to approach God in faith and ask Him to handle it. Nothing is too hard for Him. Trust that the God who stopped the sun can work a miracle in your life as well. His power is not limited by what seems realistic to you.

TODAY'S PRAYER: Father, I am grateful that no prayer is too difficult or too great for You. You make the impossible possible. Increase my faith so that I may approach You with boldness and trust. Amen

Ehud Becomes Israel's Judge

Read Judges 3:12-30

SUMMARY: Israel had been oppressed by the Moabite king for eighteen years. The Israelites sent Ehud, a left-handed man from the tribe of Benjamin, to deliver their tribute money to King Eglon of Moab. After delivering the money, Ehud told the king that he had a secret message. The king dismissed his servants, and once the two of them were alone, Ehud stabbed the king and killed him.

For much of history, being left-handed was considered unusual, and the left hand was often viewed as the weak hand. During that time, men would fasten their swords to the side opposite their dominant hand, so Ehud strapped his dagger to the right side. This detail is significant because when he approached the king, guards likely checked his left side to see if he was hiding any weapons. Because Ehud was different, he was successful at concealing his weapon and eventually killing the king.

REFLECTION: So often, we feel insecure about the things that make us different, but maybe that's what God wants to use for His will.

Is there an insecurity or perceived flaw that's holding you back? Make the decision to change your perspective today. You are not weak, strange, or overlooked. You are chosen by God to do something special. God knew what He was doing when He created you.

TODAY'S PRAYER: Father, I thank You for using what I see as imperfections for Your glory. Amen.

Jael's Victory Over Sisera

Read Judges 4

SUMMARY: There was a battle between the Israelites and the Canaanites. The Israelites were winning the battle, so Sisera, the leader of the Canaanite army, fled. A woman named Jael invited him into her tent to hide. He went into her tent and fell asleep from exhaustion. While he was sleeping, Jael took a tent peg and drove it through his head with a hammer, and he died.

God often provides us with the resources to help others, but it is our job to use them. God literally placed the enemy, Sisera, in Jael's tent. The hammer and peg were right in her reach. In that moment, Jael could have stood in fear and allowed Sisera to remain hidden. She could have waited for Barak to arrive and handle the situation. Instead, Jael knew that this was her chance to help the Israelites. God had positioned her perfectly and equipped her fully, so she seized her opportunity.

REFLECTION: God has given us all the assignment to serve others, and every day He presents opportunities, both big and small, to help someone in need. There are probably people in your life or in your community that you have considered helping but hesitated to act. If you know what someone needs and you have the means to help, then seize your opportunity. You do not have to wait for someone else to take the lead, and you do not need to wait for perfect conditions. Like Jael, act decisively and faithfully.

TODAY'S PRAYER: Father, I thank You for the gifts You have given me to serve others. Help me to be aware of the needs in my community. Give me the courage, wisdom, and obedience to act when You call me to help. Amen.

Gideon Becomes a Judge

Read Judges 6:1-24

SUMMARY: An angel of the Lord appeared to Gideon as he was hiding grain from the Midianites and told him that God had given him the task of rescuing the Israelites. Gideon immediately doubted himself, pointing to his weakness and lack of status. Because of his uncertainty, he asked God for signs to confirm that it was really God speaking to him.

Gideon is relatable not only because of his insecurity, but also because of his unresolved feelings towards God. When the angel approached Gideon and told him that the Lord was with him, Gideon's response wasn't one of relief or gratitude. Instead, he questioned God's presence, expressing hurt and confusion over Israel's suffering. There was no way that Gideon would be able to save anyone until he addressed his personal feelings toward God.

REFLECTION: Like Gideon, we may carry disappointment, doubt, or unanswered questions toward God. God invites us to be honest with Him and to bring our struggles into His presence. Pour your heart out to God and ask Him to help you rebuild any trust that has been lost. Ask Him to reveal Himself to you so that you are aware of His presence. You won't be able to move forward in your calling until your relationship with the Lord is restored.

TODAY'S PRAYER: Father, sometimes life's circumstances can shake my faith in You. I bring my doubts and disappointments before You today. I ask that You strengthen my faith and help my unbelief so that I can be fully used by You. Amen.

Gideon Destroys Baal's Altar

Read Judges 6:25-32

SUMMARY: The Lord told Gideon to destroy his father's altar to Baal and cut down the Asherah pole beside it. Then, he was to build an altar to the Lord. Gideon was instructed to use the wood from the Asherah pole as fuel for a burnt offering to the Lord. Gideon obeyed, but he did it at night out of fear. The next morning, the townspeople saw the destroyed altar and the new one. They found out that Gideon was responsible and wanted to kill him. Gideon's father, however, defended his son. He argued that Baal could defend himself if he were truly a god.

God told Gideon to tear down his father's altar—the patriarch of his family. Gideon was scared to go against his father, but he stepped out on faith and obeyed. Instead of responding with anger, his father surprised everyone by defending Gideon and openly denying Baal.

REFLECTION: There may come a time when God asks you to make difficult choices that your loved ones don't understand or approve of. He may call you to confront behavior that doesn't reflect Christ, or have uncomfortable conversations to break a generational curse. You may be scared, it may be difficult, but if God calls you to do it, then be obedient. Allow God to work on hearts, just as He did with Gideon's father. Trust God beyond the limits of your comfort zone and watch Him use your obedience to transform lives.

TODAY'S PRAYER: Father, give me courage to obey You, even when it stretches me beyond my comfort zone. Use my obedience to reveal Your truth and love to others. Amen.

Gideon and the Fleece

Read Judges 6:33-40

SUMMARY: Gideon wanted reassurance that God had called him to rescue Israel, so he asked for a sign. At Gideon's request, God made the fleece wet and the ground dry. Still unsure, Gideon asked for one more confirmation. The next morning, God made the ground wet and the fleece dry.

REFLECTION: Have you ever asked God for a sign? Many Christians hesitate to do so, feeling that it shows a lack of faith or trust. But God understands that faith is a process. Trust doesn't always come instantly—it develops over time as we learn to rely on Him. Gideon approached God with the intent of wanting to do His will, so God met Gideon in the midst of his doubt and gave him the confirmation that he needed.

There may be times when your faith fails, and you need reassurance to move forward. It is okay to ask for a sign of confirmation. God knows your heart, and He understands your desire to follow His will. Even if He doesn't grant your request in the exact way that you want, you can trust that He will find a way to give you the confirmation that you need.

TODAY'S PRAYER: Father, I thank You for being gracious and understanding towards me. It is my desire to do what is acceptable and pleasing in Your sight. I ask that You provide me with clarity and direction so that I can be obedient to Your will. Amen.

Gideon and the Midianites

Read Judges 7

SUMMARY: Gideon brought together 32,000 men to fight against the large Midianite army. The Lord had him put the men through a series of tests that eventually reduced the army to just 300. That night, Gideon and his servant went into the Midianite camp, where he received confirmation that the Lord would give Israel the victory. Gideon worshiped the Lord and then went back to the Israelite camp.

At midnight, the Israelites blew their horns, broke clay jars, and shouted. The Midianites were thrown into confusion and started to fight and kill each other. Then, Gideon sent for the warriors from several tribes of Israel to chase the Midianites away. In this way, God allowed Israel to have the victory over Midian. By making the army only a fraction of what it previously was, the people could only attribute the victory to God.

REFLECTION: Similar to the Israelites, we can be tempted to credit our success to our strength or resources. But the truth is that without God, we are nothing. Success in His plans is not measured by human standards. True victory is rooted in faith and dependence on Him.

TODAY'S PRAYER: Father, I acknowledge that my success is not through my own works but by Your power. Thank You for using me as a vessel for Your glory. Amen.

The Tribe of Ephraim Confronts Gideon

Read Judges 8:1-3

SUMMARY: The men of the tribe of Ephraim confronted Gideon because they had not been included in the initial battle against the Midianites.

Although Manasseh was the older son, Jacob blessed Ephraim first. Based on this history, the tribe of Ephraim often had a sense of entitlement over Gideon's tribe, Manasseh. When Gideon only called Ephraim to help pursue the remaining Midianites, they were offended. They questioned why they hadn't been included from the beginning. They wanted a piece of the glory.

REFLECTION: Have you ever felt upset because you weren't included in something important? Have you ever been offended because someone received praise for something you wished you had done? If so, now may be a good time to do an honest heart check. Ask yourself—were you more offended by missing the invitation, or by missing the praise? Would you feel the same way if the outcome had not been successful?

We have to be careful not to allow pride to manipulate us into thinking that we are entitled to opportunities or recognition. The truth is that we are all undeserving of the favor that we receive. God can use whomever He chooses to get the glory.

TODAY'S PRAYER: Father, I know that pride is not from You. Search my heart and remove anything within me that seeks recognition over obedience. Amen.

Gideon Kills The Kings of Midian

Read Judges 8:4-21

SUMMARY: Gideon and his 300 men were tired from chasing the Midianites, so they stopped in the town of Succoth for food. The leaders refused to help them until Gideon killed the kings of Midian. Gideon and his men caught the Midian army in a surprise attack and captured the kings and their warriors. Gideon captured a man from Succoth and had him write down the names of all the leaders in the town. He returned to Succoth with the Midianite kings, punished the leaders, and killed all the men. Gideon then killed the Midianite kings who had previously killed his brother.

Gideon's walk with God started on the right path. He was humble, growing in faith, and fully dependent on the Lord. Towards the end of his story, however, we see a shift in Gideon's character. Once humble, he was now prideful—claiming vengeance on enemies, and straying from God's plan.

REFLECTION: Sometimes we can be like Gideon. We start off humble, a willing vessel to be used by God for His glory, but if we are not careful, pride can quickly take root. Life can become more about our power and our desires rather than God's will.

Are there any areas where you may have strayed away from God's plan? If so, pray and ask God to realign your heart with His will.

TODAY'S PRAYER: Father, reveal to me any areas of my life where I may be outside of Your will. Help me to get back on track so that I can live the life that You have planned for me. Amen.

Gideon's Ephod

Read Judges 8:22-35

SUMMARY: The Israelites wanted Gideon to be their king, but he declined. Instead, he requested that everyone give him a gold earring. Gideon made an ephod from the gold and put it in his hometown. Soon, the Israelites began to worship it. Gideon returned home and had seventy sons by his many wives and one son by his concubine. When he died, the Israelites began worshiping Baal.

When Gideon made the ephod, it distracted the Israelites from the one true God and led them into idolatry. It may not have been his plan for the Israelites to start worshiping it, but that is what happened.

REFLECTION: Have you ever unintentionally caused others to fall into sin? The Bible is very clear about making sure that our lives do not become a stumbling block for others (Romans 14:13). People are watching us and looking at us as examples. We can either lead them to Christ or away from Him. Even when our intentions are good, we should pause to examine the impact of our behavior. If we notice that something in our lives is leading others away from Jesus, love requires us to let it go.

TODAY'S PRAYER: Father, I ask that You reveal to me any part of my life that could cause others to fall into sin. Help me to live a life that draws people to You. Amen.

Abimelech Becomes King

Read Judges 9:1-21

SUMMARY: Following the death of his father, Gideon, Abimelech convinced the people of Shechem to anoint him as king. After he was anointed king, he killed all of his brothers except one. Jotham, the youngest son, was the only brother to survive. He rebuked the people for making Abimelech their king and cursed them before he fled the land.

Abimelech lacked moral standards, but he had family ties to the people of Shechem. So, when it was time to choose a leader, they chose the man who served their personal agendas.

REFLECTION: What is your criteria when choosing a leader? Do you select someone with integrity and strong moral character, or are your decisions driven by what you might gain personally?

We must be careful not to select leaders who are clearly seeking power for their own prideful and selfish gain. Character matters. As believers, we are called to be discerning and intentional, seeking leaders who demonstrate the characteristics of Christ—loving their neighbors, caring for those in need, and fighting for the rights of everyone.

TODAY'S PRAYER: Father, today I lift up leaders at every level. I pray that You raise up leaders who will be selfless and make decisions for the good of everyone. Help us to not be deceived by charisma and personalities, but give us discernment to recognize the true condition of their hearts. Amen.

Shechem Rebels

Read Judges 9:22-57

SUMMARY: God allowed Abimelech to rule over Israel for three years before He sent a spirit that caused the people of Shechem to revolt. Both Abimelech's men and the people of Shechem set up ambushes for one another. After killing 1,000 people in Shechem, he attacked the town of Thebez. Abimelech appeared to be winning until a woman on the roof of a tower dropped a stone that landed on his skull. Mortally wounded, Abimelech ordered his armor bearer to end his life by sword.

In this. story, we see Jotham's curse begin to unfold. The people of Israel finally suffered the consequences of their poor decisions, and Abimelech was punished for his selfish ambitions and murderous acts. Justice was delayed, but it was not denied.

REFLECTION: Sometimes we see the evil of this world and wonder why God allows it to continue. Why do bad people get to live lavish lives? Why does it seem like power and wealth allow people to escape accountability?

This story reminds us to never get too comfortable with sin or assume that we are above correction. God is not impressed by status, charm, or wealth. Just as with Abimelech and the Israelites, everyone will eventually have to answer for their unrepentant wrongdoings.

TODAY'S PRAYER: Father, I repent for the times when I did things with evil or selfish intent. I pray that You would help me to be mindful to plant seeds of righteousness, for that is the only harvest that I want to reap. Amen.

Jephthah's Vow

Read Judges 11

SUMMARY: Jephthah led an army against the Ammonites and vowed that if God gave him the victory, he would sacrifice whatever came out of his house first to meet him upon his return. God gave Jephthah and his army the victory, but his daughter was the first to greet him when he came home. Jephthah was heartbroken, but he still sacrificed her to keep his vow.

The story of Jephthah and his daughter is difficult to process because it seems unnecessary and deeply tragic. Why did Jephthah feel the need to bargain with God? Why didn't he pause to consider the weight and potential consequences of his words?

REFLECTION: Many of us have made vows to God in the heat of the moment. "Lord, if You get me out of this speeding ticket, I'll go to church on Sunday." "Lord, if You take away this hangover, I'll never drink again." While there is nothing inherently wrong with making vows to the Lord, what we say matters.

Before making promises to God, we should ask ourselves a few questions: Will this please God? Could this harm others? Am I acting out of emotions or thoughtful obedience? God does not require reckless promises—speak with intention, and only make promises that you are prepared to keep.

TODAY'S PRAYER: Father, give me wisdom to think before I speak. Help me to make promises that honor You and do not cause harm. Guide my words so that they reflect obedience, not impulse. Amen.

The Birth of Samson

Read Judges 13

SUMMARY: There was a man named Manoah from the tribe of Dan whose wife was barren. One day, an angel appeared to Manoah's wife and told her that she would soon become pregnant. The child was going to be a Nazirite from birth, which meant that he would be set apart and sacred to God. When she shared this with Manoah, he prayed, asking God to bring the angel back so that they could receive clarity together. The Lord did as Manoah requested. When the baby was born, they named him Samson.

REFLECTION: Spiritual life is rarely meant to be walked alone. Manoah and his wife demonstrate the strength of a faithful partnership—they were united in prayer, seeking God's direction together, and trusting His plans as one.

Too often, we try to carry spiritual burdens by ourselves or make decisions without seeking counsel or sharing our hearts with a trusted partner. But God honors when we come together in faith, praying and discerning His will as a unit. When couples, friends, or family work together in spiritual alignment, they reflect God's design for community and mutual support.

TODAY'S PRAYER: Father, thank You for the gift of spiritual partnership. Help me to seek Your will together with those You have placed in my life—sharing burdens, praying in unity, and encouraging one another in faith. Amen.

Samson's Riddle

Read Judges 14

SUMMARY: Samson decided to marry a Philistine woman despite his family's wishes. At the feast before the wedding, Samson presented a riddle to thirty young men. When they were unable to figure it out, Samson's fiancée begged and pleaded until he gave her the answer. The men presented the answer to Samson, and this angered him. He killed thirty men and gave their clothing to those who solved the riddle.

Samson was physically strong but morally weak. He fell in love with someone who was appealing to the eye but did not share his values. He was determined to marry her—even though God had instructed the Israelites not to intermarry with other nations. This decision led to a lot of trouble for Samson.

REFLECTION: Have you ever heard of the term "unequally yoked?" Paul uses this term in II Corinthians 6 to explain the harm of forming close partnerships with unbelievers. Being unequally yoked doesn't just apply to marriage; it has consequences for all relationships. The people you surround yourself with influence your decisions, your mindset, and your spiritual growth. God wants us to be in community with believers who will encourage us to live in obedience and walk in our calling. He wants us to partner with people who will draw us closer in relationship with Him.

TODAY'S PRAYER: Father, I thank You for caring not only about me but also the people I allow into my life. Examine my circle and remove anyone whose influence may not be good. Surround me with like-minded believers who will draw me closer to You. Amen.

Samson's Vengeance

Read Judges 15

SUMMARY: Samson went to visit his wife, only to discover that her father had given her to another man. This angered Samson, so he used 300 foxes to burn all the Philistines' grain to the ground. When the Philistines found out the reason behind Samson's actions, they killed the woman and her father. This also angered Samson, so he attacked the Philistines and killed many of them.

Samson allowed the people of Judah to capture him and take him to the Philistines, but eventually the spirit of the Lord came upon him. He escaped and killed 1,000 Philistines. The ongoing cycle of revenge between Samson and the Philistines led to destruction and the loss of many lives.

REFLECTION: How do you respond when people treat you unfairly? Do you respond with the love of Christ, or do you match their energy? Many of us, like Samson, struggle with the need to respond to negativity with more negativity. God's Word, however, is very clear—revenge is not our responsibility. We are called to leave that to the Lord. Scripture encourages us to be like Christ and bless those who come against us (Romans 12:14). Choosing peace over retaliation is not weakness; it is obedience.

TODAY'S PRAYER: Father, thank You for Your grace that You bestow upon me even when I do things that hurt You. I ask that You help me to give that same grace to those who mistreat me. I surrender my desire for vengeance to You, and I move forward in peace. Amen.

Samson and Delilah

Read Judges 16:4-22

SUMMARY: The Philistines offered a woman named Delilah 1,100 pieces of silver to discover the source of Samson's strength. Initially, Samson lied to Delilah, but after a while, he revealed the truth. Delilah had his head shaved, and Samson was captured by the Philistines.

Delilah had proven herself to be untrustworthy. Each time Samson lied, she reported back to the Philistines, and he found himself bound and trapped. Yet, despite this clear pattern, Samson continued to share information with her, ultimately leading to his downfall.

REFLECTION: Do you have a friend or family member with a repeated history of sharing your personal business? Pay attention to the trends. If it has happened before, it is likely to happen again. Even when intentions aren't bad, careless habits can still cause serious harm. One moment of oversharing could cost you something valuable.

This is why it is important to use discernment. Before sharing something personal, you should take time to reflect: Does this person really have my best interest at heart? Have they ever shared my secrets in the past? Have they ever shared someone else's secrets with me? If your answers raise concern, take steps to protect yourself. Only share what is necessary. Take everything else to the Lord in prayer.

TODAY'S PRAYER: Father, guide my words and help me to be mindful of what I share and with whom. When I find myself wanting to overshare, remind me to give it to You instead. Amen.

Samson's Final Victory

Read Judges 16:23-31

SUMMARY: The Philistines held a feast in their temple to celebrate the capture of Samson. They brought him out and placed him between two pillars that supported the temple. God strengthened Samson, and he pushed the pillars apart. The temple crashed down, killing Samson along with the Philistines that were inside.

While Samson was imprisoned, he likely had time to reflect on his life and legacy, as well as the choices that led to his downfall. At the end of his life, he recognized one final opportunity to fulfill his calling and rescue Israel. In his death, he defeated more enemies than he had during his lifetime.

REFLECTION: How would you like to be remembered when you die? Is the way that you are currently living your life aligned with the legacy you want to leave behind? Are you making a positive impact on others? Are you walking in your calling?

While it is a morbid thought, eventually we all will die. Allow the promise of death to be an accountability partner. Let it remind you to live a life that you can be proud of—a life that is acceptable and pleasing to God.

TODAY'S PRAYER: Father, I thank You for Your promise of an abundant life, but I realize that eventually my life on earth will come to an end. Help me to seek Your kingdom first in everything that I do. I desire to live a life that brings glory to Your name. Amen.

Micah's Idols

Read Judges 17

SUMMARY: Micah confessed to his mother that he had stolen money from her. He returned the money to her, and she dedicated the coins to the Lord. She then made some of the coins into an idol. Micah placed the idol in his home, he set up a shrine for it, and he made one of his sons a priest.

One day, a young Levite man was traveling and happened to stop at Micah's house. Micah invited him to stay and made him his personal priest. He believed that God would bless him because he had a Levite as his priest. The Levite man knew that he was only supposed to be a priest for God, but chose to stay because Micah offered him money and food.

REFLECTION: Is your faith for sale? At what cost would you gain the world and lose your soul? Would you trade in your faith in God for money, physical desires, influence, or an easier lifestyle?

Life as a Christian comes with sacrifice. You have to deny yourself of your fleshly desires and surrender your life to Christ. You may not have the worldly possessions and influence, but what God offers in return is eternal and priceless. Cherish your faith and understand that it is a treasure. Don't allow the enemy to tempt you to trade your faith in God and its lifetime benefits for things that are only temporary.

TODAY'S PRAYER: Father, keep my heart from being tempted by worldly gain. Teach me to treasure my faith more than anything this world can offer. Amen.

Idolatry in the Tribe of Dan

Read Judges 18

SUMMARY: The tribe of Dan was searching for a place to settle, so they sent out warriors to explore the land. When the warriors arrived in Ephraim, they stayed at Micah's house for the night. They asked the young Levite if their journey would be successful, and he confirmed that it would be. The warriors found a good area and armed 600 men to claim it. When they came back to Micah's home, they took his sacred objects and the Levite man with them. They took over the town of Laish and lived there.

Although God had provided the tribe of Dan with land, they chose to find their own land instead. After straying away from God's plan, they eventually turned to stealing, killing, and idolatry—leaving God in their rearview.

REFLECTION: Have you ever been like the tribe of Dan—thinking that your plan was better than God's? Sometimes we forget who God is: all-knowing, all-powerful, and perfectly good. We lean on our own understanding and try to take control, only to find ourselves completely lost and in a world of sin.

This story reminds us to always choose God's plan, even when it isn't the easiest path. His will is always good, perfect, and leads to a life of abundance. Following His guidance ensures that we walk in His blessings rather than our own misguided plans.

TODAY'S PRAYER: Father, lead me and guide me along the path You have planned for my life. Help me to not stray from it. Amen.

The Levite and His Concubine

Read Judges 19

SUMMARY: In Judges 19, we find the story of a Levite's concubine. She left his home to return to her father's house. The Levite went to bring her back, and on their journey to Ephraim, a crowd of men from the tribe of Benjamin tried to sexually assault him. Instead of finding a way to make them leave, he sent his concubine out, and the men abused her until she died. Upon returning home, the Levite cut his concubine's body into twelve pieces and sent one piece to each tribe of Israel.

This story is horrifying and raises difficult questions. How did Israel reach such a point of moral decay? Why was sin so rampant?

The people of Israel had abandoned godly leadership and were doing whatever they thought was right. God's name was never mentioned in this chapter—reflecting a society where sin had become normalized, and accountability was absent.

REFLECTION: This passage serves as a warning. We must never lose sight of God or abandon godly leaders. We need to be around people who will encourage us to live a life of righteousness. We need to be familiar with God's standards and adhere to them. God is a shield to those who follow Him, but when believers turn away and tolerate sin, it opens them up to Satan's attacks.

TODAY'S PRAYER: Father, forgive me for the times when I abandoned Your Word to follow my own desires. Give me the discipline, wisdom, and courage to remain obedient to You. Amen.

The Tribe of Benjamin Captures Wives

Read Judges 20-21

SUMMARY: In Judges 20, the other Israelite tribes attacked the tribe of Benjamin because of how they had treated the Levite's concubine. They vowed not to allow their women to marry anyone from the tribe. Later, they realized that without women, the tribe of Benjamin would become extinct. In order to rectify the situation, they first provided the men with wives from Jabesh-gilead, and then they came up with a plan for the men to seize women from Shiloh who came to dance at the festival of the Lord. The men did as they were told and were able to repopulate their towns.

If you read Judges 20, you will find that the Israelites never asked God if they should fight the tribe of Benjamin—they only asked which tribe should attack first. Their choice to leave God out of their first decision led to a series of poor decisions. Only faced with near destruction did they turn to God, realizing too late that their turmoil was a direct consequence of their actions.

REFLECTION: Prioritizing our feelings over God's guidance will never give us the results that we desire. As Christians, we must consult God in everything that we do, including how we handle injustice or wrongdoing. When we seek God's guidance, we avoid unnecessary sin, chaos, and regret.

TODAY'S PRAYER: Father, I ask that Your Holy Spirit will convict me whenever I attempt to choose my feelings over Your guidance. Thank You for Your wisdom and care. Amen.

Ruth and Naomi

Read Ruth 1

SUMMARY: There was a severe famine in Israel, so a man named Elimelech moved with his family to Moab. After they had settled there, Elimelech died. His wife Naomi was left with her two sons. The two sons married Moabite women, Orpah and Ruth. A few years later, both of Naomi's sons died, so she decided to move back to Judah. Orpah decided to stay in Moab, but Ruth stayed with Naomi and went to Judah.

Naomi hadn't done anything wrong, and yet she was in a situation that seemed a lot like punishment. Upon arriving back home, she asked to be called Mara, meaning bitter, because she felt that the Lord had made life bitter for her. Still, God had not abandoned her. God provided Naomi with a daughter-in-law to have her back and play a huge role in restoring her joy.

REFLECTION: It is important during our moments of grief and disappointment to acknowledge those who stick beside us through thick and thin. Ruth was mourning the loss of a husband, but she was still there to support Naomi. In the same way, we are all going through our own battles and challenges, so it takes a special person to make an effort to consider the needs of others. Don't overlook the people who show up for you when life is hard. Take time to thank them for being a true friend.

TODAY'S PRAYER: Father, thank You for blessing me with genuine friends. Help me to never take them for granted. Show me ways that I can be a better friend. Amen.

Ruth and Boaz

Read Ruth 2

SUMMARY: Once Ruth and Naomi arrived in Bethlehem, Ruth decided to find work picking up stalks of grain in the harvest fields. She ended up working in the field of a man named Boaz, who was a relative of her late father-in-law. When Boaz found out who Ruth was and how she had looked after Naomi, he took measures to make sure that she was safe, fed, and cared for while she worked.

It's safe to say that Ruth was a woman of good character. We've already discussed her selfless act of leaving Moab to go with Naomi, but in this story, we see that she continued to remain loyal to Naomi once they arrived in Bethlehem. In Bethlehem, she worked in the fields to provide for herself and her mother-in-law. Word spread about Ruth's kindness to the point that she captured the attention of Boaz. Boaz chose to show kindness to Ruth because of her kindness to Naomi.

REFLECTION: It is so important to be men and women of integrity. When we treat people with kindness and have good intentions, people take notice. More importantly, God sees our faithfulness and honors those who choose to help others.

TODAY'S PRAYER: Father, fill my heart with kindness and compassion so that my life reflects Your love to those around me. Amen.

Ruth Goes to the Threshing Floor

Read Ruth 3

SUMMARY: Naomi wanted Ruth to have a secure future, and she felt that Boaz could provide that for her. She gave Ruth instructions on how to approach Boaz privately and make her request known. Ruth approached Boaz as he was asleep on the threshing floor. When Boaz awoke and heard Ruth's appeal, he wanted to help, but there was another man who was more closely related to Ruth and Naomi. Boaz could not marry Ruth unless this man gave up his right to her. Boaz told Ruth that he would handle the situation and instructed her to leave discreetly so no one would know she had been there.

Going to the threshing floor to meet Boaz was likely an anxiety-inducing situation for Ruth. She had no idea how Boaz would respond. He could have taken advantage of her in that private moment, or he could have rejected her. Regardless, Ruth understood that without a husband, her future and Naomi's were uncertain. Trusting Naomi's guidance, she humbly lay at Boaz's feet.

REFLECTION: Oftentimes, we, like Ruth, can find ourselves facing uncertain futures and situations outside of our control. In those moments, the best thing that we can do is to humble ourselves and sit at the Lord's feet. Make your petition to the Lord. Surrender your concerns and worries to Him. Be confident that He can handle whatever you give to Him.

TODAY'S PRAYER: Father, help me to always remember that in times of trouble, the safest place I can be is at Your feet, surrendering my cares to You. Amen.

Boaz Marries Ruth

Read Ruth 4

SUMMARY: Boaz spoke with the close relative, whom he had mentioned. The relative willingly surrendered his rights to Ruth and to Naomi's husband's land, allowing Boaz to redeem both. Boaz and Ruth married, and Ruth gave birth to a son named Obed. Naomi helped care for the child as if he were her own. In time, Obed became the grandfather of King David.

The marriage of Boaz and Ruth didn't just bless them; it also brought restoration to Naomi. In Ruth 1, Naomi was depressed. She had lost her family, and she had left the place that had been her home for years. She told everyone to call her Mara. In Ruth 4, however, we see a transformed Naomi. Her plan for Ruth's future was successful, her family line was preserved, and she had a grandson to love on. In this new season, Naomi experienced God as a restorer.

REFLECTION: Life will not always be perfect. There will be seasons of loss, grief, confusion, and unanswered questions. In those moments, reflect on the story of Naomi. It is okay to mourn what you have lost, but don't lose sight of hope. Whatever has been taken—joy, peace, purpose, or stability—God can restore it.

TODAY'S PRAYER: Father, I pray that You remove any hurt, bitterness, grudges, or anger that I have in my heart. Replace it with Your peace and joy, and help me to trust You as my restorer. Amen.

Hannah Prays for a Son

Read I Samuel 1:1-2:11

SUMMARY: Hannah was a woman who was loved by her husband, but the Lord kept her from having children. For years, her husband's other wife mocked her infertility, causing her great pain. One day, Hannah went to the Tabernacle and vowed to God that if He gave her a son, she would give the son back to the Lord. After praying, she was no longer sad.

At a certain point in the story, it seems like Hannah realized that her barrenness was not about her, but all about God. She promised God that if He blessed her with a son, she would give her son back to Him. Not only was Hannah blessed with her son Samuel, but after she gave him to God, the Lord blessed her with five more children (I Samuel 2:21).

REFLECTION: Think about a time when you felt disappointed with God. In retrospect, was there a purpose behind the pain? In moments of disappointment, it's easy to get caught up in the emotion of the situation. You feel hurt. You feel rejected. You don't understand what's going on. But perhaps, in those moments, you should take the focus off of yourself, and change your perspective to how God might get the glory in the situation. Maybe the Lord wants you to learn to trust Him more, maybe God is strengthening you for a new season, or maybe God is using you as an example for someone else. There is always a purpose behind the pain.

TODAY'S PRAYER: Father, I know that I may not always understand Your ways, but please give me the grace I need to continue trusting You through the process. Amen.

Eli's Sons

Read I Samuel 2:12-36

SUMMARY: Eli had two sons, Hophni and Phinehas. They disrespected the Lord and did not take their roles as priests seriously. Eli was aware that his sons were wicked, and he told them to stop, but they did not listen. One day, a man of God came and rebuked Eli for honoring his sons more than God. He declared that the Lord would put an end to Eli's family line, Hophni and Phinehas would die on the same day, and that another family would take over their roles as priests.

While Eli was not directly responsible for his sons' wickedness, his failure was in how he responded to it. Although he warned them, he never disciplined them when they ignored his rebuke. He continued to allow them to serve as priests without any consequences for their actions.

REFLECTION: Eli's story reminds us that there are consequences to passively allowing people under our authority to disrespect God. We are not to put anything before God, and that includes the feelings of others. Correction should always be done in love, but obedience must come first. When we are faithful to address wrongdoing, we can trust God to handle the outcome.

TODAY'S PRAYER: Father, help me to never fear anyone more than I fear You. Give me the strength and wisdom to correct those under my authority in love. Amen.

The Lord Speaks to Samuel

Read I Samuel 3

SUMMARY: Samuel was awakened from his sleep by a voice calling his name and assumed that it was Eli. Eli denied that it was him and told Samuel to go back to bed. After it happened three times, Eli realized that it was the Lord calling Samuel. He told Samuel that if it happened again, he should say, "Speak Lord; for thy servant heareth."

Eli helped Samuel to recognize the voice of God and showed him how to respond. Eli told Samuel to go back to bed. In this way, he could make himself available to God. Samuel's bed was a quiet place away from distractions so that he could clearly hear what God had to say. Next, Eli told Samuel to come to God humbly. Samuel acknowledged that he was God's servant. In this way, he demonstrated his readiness to listen and obey whatever God instructed him to do.

REFLECTION: Sometimes, it can be difficult to discern whether we are hearing the voice of God or the noise of the world around us. Learning to recognize God's voice takes time and practice. Thankfully, God understands that we are learning and extends grace. When God wanted to speak with Samuel, He did not stop trying after the first or second attempt. He continued calling until Samuel figured out that it was God speaking to him. When God has a message for you, you can trust that He will not stop calling until you recognize His voice.

TODAY'S PRAYER: Father, help me to recognize Your voice. Silence anything that distracts me from hearing You. Amen.

The Death of Eli and His Sons

Read I Samuel 4

SUMMARY: Israel was losing a battle with the Philistines, so they decided to bring the Ark of the Covenant into battle with them. They still lost the battle, and the Israelites who survived the battle fled the scene. The Ark of the Covenant was captured, and Eli's sons were killed. When Eli found out that his sons had been killed and the Ark of the Covenant was captured, he fell backward from his seat, broke his neck, and died.

Israel's leadership—specifically the priests—had continued to sin with no remorse, but when it was time for battle, they called on God and sent out the Ark of the Covenant like a good luck charm. They wanted God to be present in times of trouble, but they did not have a desire for God when things were going well.

REFLECTION: Sometimes, as Christians, we can behave the same way. During difficult seasons, we cling to God. Our prayer life is consistent, we're reading the Bible, and we're going to church every Sunday. But when life gets better, our devotion can fade. We become less intentional about seeking God, we ignore His commands, and we go back to leaning on our own understanding.

God desires daily connection, not emergency devotion. Let us seek His presence not because of what He can do for us, but simply because of who He is.

TODAY'S PRAYER: Father, I come to You today just to say thank You. It is a privilege to be in Your presence. I honor You today and always. Amen.

The Philistines Capture the Ark

Read I Samuel 5

SUMMARY: The Philistines captured the Ark of the Covenant and took it into the temple of their god, Dagon. When they returned the next morning, they found that the idol of Dagon had fallen in front of the Ark. The next morning, the idol had fallen again—this time broken. After that, the Lord sent tumors on the people in the town of Ashdod and the surrounding villages. Every time the Philistines moved the Ark of the Covenant to a new city, a plague of tumors would follow.

Imagine the Philistines' surprise when they placed the Ark of the Covenant beside the idol of Dagon and found the idol on the ground, not once, but twice. God was making a statement: there are no gods equal to Him, and none greater. If the Philistines missed the message at first, then they certainly understood His power when the plagues began.

REFLECTION: Are there things in your life that you are putting on the same level as God—social media, money, or even friends and family? Is there something that is taking up time or resources that should be given to Him? The Bible says that no man can serve two masters (Matthew 6:24). Eventually, you will have to make a choice. Today, make the choice to serve God alone.

TODAY'S PRAYER: Father, I recognize that sometimes I put things before You. Please forgive me. Today, I choose to put You first in everything that I do. Amen.

The Philistines Return the Ark

Read I Samuel 6

SUMMARY: The Philistines were advised by their priests and wise men to return the Ark of the Covenant to the Israelites along with guilt offerings. They placed the Ark and the gifts on a new cart pulled by two cows. They decided that if the cows went to Beth-shemesh, then the plagues they suffered were from the Lord. The cows went straight to Beth-shemesh, confirming God's hand in the matter.

When the Ark arrived, the people of Beth-shemesh rejoiced and offered sacrifices. Yet, seventy men were struck down for looking into the Ark. Instead of learning how to honor God properly, the people chose the easier path and asked that the Ark be moved to Kiriath-jearim. This response highlights how natural it is to reject holiness when it becomes too much of a burden.

REFLECTION: Do you look at holiness as a burden? Do you find yourself so content in your sinful ways that any positive change to your lifestyle seems inconvenient? Regardless of your sin, it can be hard to step away from what you are accustomed to and choose righteousness, but that is what God requires of us. His word tells us specifically to be holy because He is holy (Leviticus 11:44).

Take time today to reflect on areas where you may have chosen comfort over righteousness. Make the decision to live fully for God.

TODAY'S PRAYER: Father, forgive me for choosing convenience over holiness. Give me the strength to make the necessary changes to live for You. Amen.

Samuel Leads Israel to Victory

Read I Samuel 7:1-11

SUMMARY: The Israelites were in the process of removing their idols and turning back to the Lord when they found out that the Philistines were approaching to attack. They begged Samuel to continue praying to God to save them from the Philistines. Samuel sacrificed a lamb to the Lord and continued to pray. The Philistines arrived ready to attack, but the Lord spoke from heaven, and it confused them. The Israelites chased the Philistines and killed them.

REFLECTION: When you decide to make a personal change and give your life to Christ, it does not change the world around you. There are still problems that you will have to face and overcome. Look at the Israelites; they had people ready to attack them while they were in the middle of fasting. The good thing is that the Israelites had the wisdom to turn to God and ask for help.

Life's circumstances can be stressful and intimidating, but they don't have to overpower our faith. In moments of fear, seek God. Don't be afraid to ask someone to intercede on your behalf. Remember that the same God who rescued the Israelites is with you. Just like He protected them, He will protect you. See moments of trouble as opportunities to exercise your faith. As you grow in faith, you gradually remove fear.

TODAY'S PRAYER: Father, when fear rises and opposition comes, remind me to turn to You first. Help me to trust You in the middle of the battle and not rely on my own strength. Give me the humility to ask for prayer and the faith to believe that You are fighting for me. Amen.

Israel Requests a King

Read I Samuel 8

SUMMARY: Samuel's sons were corrupt and failed to take their role as judges seriously, which upset the Israelites. Instead of trusting God to handle the situation, the elders of Israel asked for a king to lead them like other nations. Samuel warned them of the consequences of choosing human leadership over God, but they didn't listen. The Lord allowed them to have a king.

God had established a system where the Israelites were led by judges chosen and empowered by Him. After years of being under that leadership, the Israelites rejected what God designed, believing life would be better if they followed the pattern of other nations. They soon learned that choosing comparison over obedience leads to disappointment.

REFLECTION: The Israelites believed their lives would be better if they looked like the nations around them. We fall into the same pattern when comparison begins to shape our decisions. When we measure our lives against others, we can become dissatisfied with what God has given us and tempted to step outside His will. Comparison often promises fulfillment, but it rarely delivers it. Obedience, on the other hand, may require patience and trust, but it always keeps us aligned with God's purpose. True peace is found not in keeping up with others, but in faithfully following God where He has placed us.

TODAY'S PRAYER: Father, help me to choose obedience over imitation and faith over dissatisfaction. Align my heart with Your will and guard me from the disappointment that comes from comparison. Amen.

Saul is Anointed as King

Read I Samuel 10:1-16

SUMMARY: Samuel took a flask of olive oil and poured it over Saul's head to anoint him as king, and then he kissed him as a sign of his own approval. To prove to Saul that God had chosen him to be king, Samuel told Saul of several signs that he should look for. Saul saw the confirmations, but still refused to reveal his new role to his family.

Notice that although Saul was anointed by Samuel, his transformation did not occur until he left, and the Spirit of the Lord came upon him. While Samuel was a trusted spiritual mentor, it was the Lord who had the power. Samuel could offer advice and pray for Saul, but only God could transform him.

REFLECTION: We must be careful to not put our spiritual leaders in the place of God. We should not depend on them more than we do on our Savior. So often, we look to prophets and preachers for clarity when we have full access to God and the Bible. We run to our pastor for prayer without taking time to pray on our own. At the end of the day, our spiritual leaders are still human. They cannot change our hearts. They cannot transform our lives. Only God can. Continue to fellowship with other believers, but make it a point to seek God first in everything that you do.

TODAY'S PRAYER: Father, I am grateful for the circle of believers that You have placed in my life, but I acknowledge that You alone are God. Help me to never put anyone before You. Amen.

Saul Revealed as King

Read I Samuel 10:17-27

SUMMARY: Saul had already been chosen by God and anointed by Samuel to be king, but it was finally time for it to be publicly announced. Samuel called a meeting of all the people of Israel. The tribe of Benjamin was chosen by process of elimination, then the family of Matrites was singled out, and finally Saul, son of Kish, was chosen. The people looked for Saul, and the Lord told them that Saul was hiding among the baggage. They brought him out, and Samuel announced him as king.

REFLECTION: God loves to stretch us and take us out of our comfort zones to serve Him. He has a habit of calling us to do things that we never imagined that we would do. When God calls you to do something uncomfortable, do you immediately get to work, or do you hide in your "baggage?" Maybe your "baggage" is imposter syndrome, or your limitations, or fear of the unknown. You can try to hide from God, but He sees all. If you don't step out voluntarily, He will find a way to bring you out. Take the initiative to come out of your hiding place and trust God to be with you through your journey.

TODAY'S PRAYER: Father, I ask You to show me if I'm hiding from what You have called me to do. Please give me the courage to step out and accept Your plan for my life. Even if I am uncomfortable with the task, I trust that You will be with me and Your plans will never fail. Amen.

Samuel Rebukes Saul

Read I Samuel 13

SUMMARY: Saul's son Jonathan had defeated the Philistines. After the news spread, the Philistines put together a large army against the Israelites. This caused the Israelites to panic. Samuel instructed Saul to stay where he was for seven days, and he would come to sacrifice a burnt offering. Saul waited seven days, and Samuel still wasn't there, so Saul decided to sacrifice the burnt offering himself. When Samuel arrived, he rebuked Saul and told him that his kingdom would end.

The thought of being outnumbered by a large Philistine army intimidated the Israelites. They began to scatter and hide out of fear. Saul did as he was told and waited the seven days, but when he didn't see Samuel, he panicked. His fear led him to take matters into his own hands and disobey God by offering a burnt sacrifice on his own.

REFLECTION: It is easy to trust God when everything is going as planned, and everything falls into the expected timeline, but what happens when it doesn't? Do you respond in fear or do you trust in God's faithfulness? Saul's fear caused him to act prematurely, costing him God's favor. As a result, God sought out someone else from a different bloodline to be Israel's next king. Don't allow your fear to ruin your legacy. If you are struggling with fear, ask God to strengthen your faith.

TODAY'S PRAYER: Father, forgive me for the times that I let fear guide my actions. I ask that You replace my fear with faith in You. Amen.

Jonathan's Plan

Read I Samuel 14:1-23

SUMMARY: Jonathan secretly went with his armor bearer to scout the Philistine camp. After asking for and receiving a sign from God that He would give them the victory, the two men entered into battle and killed twenty men. Saul's lookouts noticed that the Philistines were starting to disappear, so Saul and his men entered into battle. The Lord gave Israel the victory that day.

Jonathan knew that he was outnumbered by the Philistines, but he had strong faith in God. He knew that was enough to win the battle. Jonathan still asked for God's confirmation before he fought. He understood that although God has all power, it might not be within His will, and he didn't want to fight without God's approval.

REFLECTION: While it's important to have faith, it's just as important to check with God to make sure that what you're asking is within His will. Yes, He could give you that dream job, but perhaps He wants you to go a different route. Yes, God could give you a bigger house, but perhaps He wants you to take better care of the one you have. God has all power and this includes the power to say "no." So before you assume that God will use His power to do something for you, make sure that your plan aligns with His.

TODAY'S PRAYER: Father, I thank You that You have all power in Your hands. I ask that You guide my decision-making. Give me discernment to know whether or not what I desire to do is within Your will. I trust You. Amen.

Saul's Foolish Oath

Read I Samuel 14:24-46

SUMMARY: Saul ordered the Israelite army to fast in preparation for their battle against the Philistines. He said that any man who ate would be put to death. Jonathan was not present when Saul gave the instructions, so he ate some honey. When Saul found out, he was ready to kill his son, but the people intervened and saved Jonathan.

It is important to point out that God never called for the Israelite army to fast. That was Saul's doing. And because it was a self-imposed rule that only sounded good, it backfired. The Israelites obeyed Saul's order, but the fast made them weak in battle. Then, when it was finally time to end the fast, their hunger caused them to sin against the Lord by eating unclean meat. Not only that, his oath put his son at risk of being killed.

REFLECTION: As Christians, we can sometimes be like Saul and impose rules on people with no spiritual backing. Before speaking out against something or enforcing a rule, we should pause and ask ourselves: Did God truly instruct me to do this? Am I interpreting Scripture correctly? God honors obedience that comes from His will, not rules we make up on our own.

TODAY'S PRAYER: Father, forgive me for times that I valued rules over Your guidance. Please help me to remember to consult You before acting on what I think is right. Protect me from people who would lead me to engage in practices that have no spiritual value. Amen.

Saul is Rejected as King

Read I Samuel 15

SUMMARY: God instructed Saul to completely destroy the Amalekites and all of their possessions because of how they had treated the Israelites. Saul, however, only partially obeyed. He saved some of the animals and did not kill the king. As a result of Saul's disobedience, God rejected him as king.

God had given Saul specific instructions, but Saul decided to obey what worked for him. He argued that he only sinned a little and his intentions were to give a sacrifice to the Lord. What Saul failed to realize was that the Lord knew his heart. He knew that Saul made his decisions based on selfish gain. When Samuel went to find Saul, Saul was setting up a monument to himself. By sparing the king, he could make a public spectacle of his killing and win the approval of the people. By sacrificing the animals, he would still be able to eat and enjoy them. His intentions were for self and self alone.

REFLECTION: If we say that we are Christians, we cannot pick and choose which parts of God's Word to obey. Claiming to serve God while putting your will above His is a sin. It's actually idolatry because you are glorifying yourself. Let us be intentional about serving God wholly. He is deserving of our full obedience.

TODAY'S PRAYER: Father, I confess that sometimes I choose my desires over Your will. I repent now and ask for Your forgiveness. Give me the wisdom to follow Your ways and not my own. Amen.

David is Anointed as King

Read I Samuel 16:1-13

SUMMARY: The Lord instructed Samuel to anoint one of Jesse's sons to be Israel's next king. When Samuel arrived at Jesse's home, he passed by all of the sons that were present, but the Lord had not chosen any of them. Samuel asked if Jesse had any other sons, and he mentioned that he had one more tending to the livestock, David. Jesse called David in, and he was anointed to be the next king.

When Samuel arrived at Jesse's home, he automatically assumed that Jesse's son Eliab would be chosen as the king because of his appearance. Jesse only presented his older sons to Samuel because he assumed that one of them would be the king. Both men were wrong. God was not concerned about the external factors—He was focused on the heart.

REFLECTION: Have you ever compared yourself to others and felt unworthy of God's calling? Perhaps they sang better, prayed better, or had more knowledge of God's Word. The truth is that if you keep living, you are bound to find someone better than you at something. That does not mean that you have to count yourself out. God looks past the outside and directly at your heart. Don't allow self-doubt to creep in. You may think that you are not the best choice, but God believes in you. Ask Him to help you see yourself as He sees you.

TODAY'S PRAYER: Father, I thank You for the gifts that You have given me. Forgive me for the times that I doubted my worth because I compared myself to others. I ask that You help me to see myself and my gifts in the way that You see me. Amen.

David Serves Saul

Read I Samuel 16:14-23

SUMMARY: King Saul was experiencing depression and fear, so his servants suggested that David come and play the harp for him. David went as requested and began playing for him. Saul appreciated David and made him his armor bearer.

After David was anointed to be King, he didn't automatically step into his new role. Instead, he became a servant for Saul. David did not grumble about the fact that he was supposed to be the king. He remained humble and served with excellence. He waited patiently for his opportunity.

REFLECTION: Sometimes when God promises us something, we expect to receive it immediately, but that is not always the case. There are many stories in the Bible where God gave a promise or called someone to do something, and then they were required to wait for years.

We have to remember, however, that each step in our journey is preparing us for what we are waiting for. When David was the armor bearer, it gave him a chance to see the responsibilities of the king first-hand. That way, when it was his turn, he knew what to expect.

Learn to wait like David and have faith that your time will come. Trust the process and use every opportunity as preparation for the future.

TODAY'S PRAYER: Father, I thank You for preparing me for what You have planned for me. Please help me to remain positive during my waiting season. I want to learn and grow so that I will be fully equipped for whatever is next. Amen.

David and Goliath

Read I Samuel 17

SUMMARY: While visiting the army camp, David heard the Philistine giant Goliath taunting Israel and volunteered to fight him. Refusing armor, David knocked out Goliath with a stone and a sling. Then David killed Goliath with Goliath's own sword. The rest of the Philistines ran away in fear.

David had every reason to avoid Goliath's challenge. David was young and wasn't even part of the army. The only reason he had come to the Israelite camp was to deliver food to his brothers. It would have been easy to allow the naysayers to discourage him. They meant well. They just didn't want David to be killed. David, however, trusted God. He knew that he did not have the strength to kill Goliath on his own, but he trusted that God would be there with him just as He had in the past.

REFLECTION: We should learn from David that there will be moments when we do not measure up on our own. Our confidence does not come from our strength—it comes from knowing that God is with us. Just like David had fought bears and lions in the past, we can reflect on our past and see how God has prepared us for the moment at hand. Let that be your encouragement to face the "giants" in your life.

TODAY'S PRAYER: Father, help me to use the gifts You have given me to tackle the troubles in my life with courage. I know that no problem is too big or difficult with You by my side. Amen.

Saul is Jealous of David

Read I Samuel 18:1-16

SUMMARY: As David was returning home after one of his conquests, the women came out and danced for joy, singing his praises. This upset Saul and caused him to be jealous of David. The next day, Saul became manic. As usual, David played his harp in an attempt to soothe Saul, but it did not work. Saul hurled spears at David twice, intending to pin him to the wall, but David escaped.

Saul still maintained his position as the king, but the Lord's presence had left him, deeply affecting his mental health. Instead of repenting and seeking God for help, Saul turned to alternative remedies. He tried to soothe his depression and paranoia with music.

REFLECTION: When your mental health is suffering, do you go to the Lord first, or do you look for alternative methods? While there is nothing wrong with seeking out help from other sources, we should never prioritize alternative or temporary methods over God. Go to therapy and go to church. Listen to music, but also take time to meditate on the Lord. Take your medications, but don't forget to pray. In whatever you do, always seek God first. He has control over everything, including your nervous system, and He can give you peace that surpasses understanding.

TODAY'S PRAYER: Father, today I seek Your help regarding my mental health. Fill me with Your peace and love. Give me wisdom so that I may receive the help I need. Amen.

Jonathan is a Friend to David

Read I Samuel 19:1-10

SUMMARY: Jonathan told David about Saul's plan to kill him. The next day, Jonathan went to Saul and spoke well of David. He reminded Saul of how David had been helpful and slain Goliath. He reminded Saul of David's innocence. Saul assured Jonathan that he would not kill David. It seemed as if everything was resolved, but one day, as David was playing his harp, Saul attempted to kill David with his spear, but David escaped.

Jonathan knew that he was technically next in line to be king, but he respected the fact that God had anointed David for the role. Instead of being angry with David or jealous of his anointing, he stood by David and was concerned about his safety. He spoke well of David to his father and did his best to stop Saul from killing him.

REFLECTION: How do you respond when your friend gets an honor or promotion that you feel you deserve? Do you encourage them, or do you become jealous and distant? It can be hard to witness the people in your circle living the life that you expected to have or having the influence that you desired, but a true friend celebrates and doesn't compete. When we trust that God's plan for us is secure, we can support others without resentment. If you're struggling to be happy for your friends, ask God to help you shift your perspective—from envy to gratitude—and to give you the grace to love faithfully, even when it's difficult.

TODAY'S PRAYER: Father, help me to be a faithful friend. Remove jealousy from my heart and teach me to celebrate others with sincerity and love. Help me to trust that what You have for me will come in Your perfect time. Amen.

Michal Protects David

Read I Samuel 19:11-24

SUMMARY: Saul sent troops to David's house with the intention of killing him, but his wife, Michal, helped him to escape by lowering him through a window. She used an idol as a decoy and put it in David's bed, buying him time to flee. When the troops came, they initially thought that the idol was David, sick and resting in bed, but they soon discovered that Michal had lied. When Saul questioned Michal about lying, she pretended that David had threatened to kill her. David escaped safely and went to live with Samuel.

It seems as if David was unaware of the impending doom that awaited him, but thankfully, his wife, Michal, was prepared. In no time, she assessed the situation, put together a plan for David's escape, and determined how she would protect herself as well. All David had to do was trust her plan and follow her instructions.

REFLECTION: There are times when we may not recognize the danger around us, but thankfully, we serve a God who is aware of everything. Before we even see the trouble, He already has a plan in place. God often uses people and unexpected means to protect and deliver us. Our role is to trust His plan and obey His direction, even when it doesn't make sense.

TODAY'S PRAYER: Father, thank You for watching over me at all times. I can have peace knowing that I am safe in Your loving hands. Amen.

Jonathan Protects David

Read I Samuel 20

SUMMARY: David was convinced that Saul still intended to kill him, but Jonathan was unsure. They devised a plan to test Saul's reaction to David's absence at the new moon festival. Saul's anger confirmed David's fears. He even tried to kill Jonathan. Jonathan warned David as planned, and the two parted ways.

In I Samuel 19:6, Saul vowed to Jonathan that he would not kill David, so Jonathan initially struggled to believe David's concern. Still, he listened. Though conflicted, Jonathan chose loyalty and stood by his friend.

REFLECTION: Are you the kind of friend that Jonathan was to David—loyal, honest, and supportive? Do you offer your friends empathy even when you don't fully understand what they are going through? As we get older, it can sometimes get harder to be the friend that you would truly like to be. Your friends may not live near you. You may have less time to spend with them due to your family or career, but meaningful friendships require intentional effort. You should be there for your friends in some way, shape, or form, especially when they are in need.

This week, reach out to a friend in a simple but meaningful way. Let them know that they are seen, valued, and supported.

TODAY'S PRAYER: Father, I thank You for the friends that You have placed in my life. Help me to love them well and to be present, supportive, and compassionate. Amen.

Hidden in the Wilderness

Read I Samuel 23:13-29

SUMMARY: David heard that Saul knew of his whereabouts, so he, along with his 600 men, hid in the wilderness. Saul searched for David, but God would not allow Saul to find him. Jonathan, however, found David and reassured him that God would keep His promise and make him the next king of Israel. At a certain point, Saul was close to finding David as they were on opposite sides of a mountain, but Saul received a message that the Philistines were raiding Israel, and he went back home.

It's kind of hard to picture 600 men being able to successfully hide from anyone, but the Bible says that God kept the men hidden from Saul. People literally gave Saul their location, but no matter how hard Saul tried, the men remained out of his grasp.

REFLECTION: Like David, God may place us in a hidden season to protect and prepare us for what's ahead. Being hidden can feel frustrating, lonely, or discouraging, but it is often where God refines us and strengthens our faith. Trust that His timing is intentional. Stepping into your calling without His covering can lead to failure, but waiting and remaining hidden for a season allows His work to be complete.

TODAY'S PRAYER: Father, while at times I get impatient, I recognize the importance of being hidden. I thank You for Your protection as You prepare me for my purpose. Allow me to rest in You and trust Your timing. Amen.

David Spares Saul's Life

Read I Samuel 24

SUMMARY: Saul took 3,000 men and went to search for David and his men. As he was on the journey, he went into a cave to relieve himself. Saul just so happened to enter the cave where David and his men were hiding. David's men encouraged him to seize the moment and kill Saul, but David declined. He cut off a piece of the hem of Saul's robe and then left him alone. Once Saul left, David came out and showed him the fabric to prove that he had spared his life.

It can be easy to see why David's men thought that Saul's presence in the cave was a sign from God to kill him. David, however, was a man after God's own heart. It wasn't that he respected Saul, but he loved and respected the God who chose Saul to be king. To kill Saul would be a sin against God.

REFLECTION: Have you ever felt mistreated by others? How did you respond? Did you retaliate or attempt to fight back? We honor God when we exercise self-control when dealing with others. We demonstrate God's love when we choose to be kind to those who attempt to harm us. Choose to approach all relationships with self-control and compassion. It won't be easy, but we have the example of David and even Jesus to model our response after.

TODAY'S PRAYER: Father, I ask that You give me the discipline to exercise self-control in moments where I desire to retaliate. I want the way that I treat others to be a reflection of Your compassion and love. Amen.

Nabal Angers David

Read I Samuel 25:1-38

SUMMARY: While in the wilderness, David's men asked a wealthy man named Nabal to share his resources with them. Even though David's men had treated Nabal's men and their flocks well, Nabal refused. David became angry and planned to kill him, but Nabal's wife, Abigail, intervened. Because of her wisdom, David spared Nabal's life.

Some people can be so obsessed with their own lives that they have little to no regard for the well-being of others. Nabal was that guy. He was so focused on *his* bread, *his* water, and *his* meat that he slaughtered for *his* shearers that he didn't take into consideration the help that David and his men had provided freely. His pride and lack of concern for others nearly brought destruction upon his household.

REFLECTION: We cannot serve a generous God while living selfishly. We must be cognizant that nothing that we have is ours alone, but rather everything is a gift from God. There is a world full of people who need our help—the poor, the sick, the lonely. Instead of exhibiting traits of Nabal, let's show them Jesus. Offer them compassion, love, and kindness.

TODAY'S PRAYER: Father, forgive me for the times that I have been selfish with the blessings that You gave me. Help me to have a giving heart. Amen.

David Spares Saul Again

Read I Samuel 26

SUMMARY: Once again, Saul took 3,000 men into the wilderness to find David. One night, David and Abishai went into Saul's camp and found him sleeping. Abishai urged David to kill Saul, but David refused and took some of Saul's belongings instead. David waited until he was a safe distance away and showed Saul and his men that he had once again spared his life.

In I Samuel 24, we found David and Saul in a similar predicament, and Saul appeared to be remorseful. But in I Samuel 26, the Ziphanites had revealed David's hiding place, and Saul was once again ready to attack. The guilt and conviction that he once felt were a thing of the past.

REFLECTION: Are you like Saul when you commit sins? Do you have a tendency to feel remorseful in the moment but then soon return to your old ways? As Christians, we have to be intentional about not just feeling sorry in the moment, but actually allowing the conviction to lead to change. It is not okay to resume your old ways once the feelings of sorrow and regret leave. There needs to be some action behind your words. Yes, God is merciful towards us and quick to forgive, but when you take His love for granted, it takes a toll on your relationship with Him. Repentance isn't always the easy choice, but it is the right one.

TODAY'S PRAYER: Father, let my convictions be the catalyst for change in my life. Amen.

Saul Consults a Medium

Read I Samuel 28

SUMMARY: The Philistines were preparing to fight Israel again. Saul was afraid and asked the Lord what he should do, but the Lord did not answer. In fear, Saul disguised himself and went to a medium, who summoned Samuel. Samuel told Saul that the Philistines would defeat the Israelites and kill him. This greatly upset Saul.

Saul had banished all wizards and mediums from the land, but when he didn't hear from God, he panicked and turned to witchcraft for help. What he received was a response that he didn't want to hear.

REFLECTION: Although we can all judge Saul for going to see a medium, we can probably relate to him as well. How often do we go to God for clarity on a situation and then panic when we don't get an answer? How often do we decide to take matters into our own hands if we don't immediately hear from God?

Sometimes God is silent because He wants to see if you will continue to follow Him without all the answers. Don't panic and run to different worldly sources for clarity. Trust Him. Wait on Him. Acknowledge Him, and He will direct your path (Proverbs 3:5-6).

TODAY'S PRAYER: Father, help me to trust You even when I don't have clarity. Give me patience to wait on You and faith to follow You. Amen.

David Destroys the Amalekites

Read I Samuel 30

SUMMARY: While David and his men were away, the Amalekites went to Ziklag and raided their homes. David asked God if he should chase after the raiders, and God promised David success. David and 600 men set out to find the Amalekites, but 200 men were unable to continue the journey due to exhaustion. David and the 400 men who were left continued their pursuit.

When David and his men reached the Amalekites, they killed most of the men and recovered everything that they had lost in the raid. On the way back home, they ran into the 200 men who had been left behind. Some of the 400 did not want to share what they had recovered, but David told them not to be selfish with what the Lord had given them.

REFLECTION: What David and the 400 men had received was not because of their works, but because of the hand of God on their lives. It is not God's desire for us to be selfish with what He has given us, especially when He has blessed us in abundance, and we are aware of a need. Let us choose to be like David and bless others. When we steward what God has given us well, then He can trust us with more.

TODAY'S PRAYER: Father, I ask that You remove any selfish desires that I have so that I can be a blessing to others. Amen.

The Death of Saul and His Sons

Read I Samuel 31:1- II Samuel 1:16

SUMMARY: The Philistines attacked Israel and killed three of Saul's sons —Jonathan, Abinadab, and Malkishua. Saul had been wounded greatly, but he begged his armor bearer to kill him before the Philistines could do so. The armor bearer was afraid to kill him, so Saul fell on his own sword. An Amalekite man came to David and told him about the death of Saul and Jonathan. The Amalekite took credit for Saul's death. David then instructed his men to kill the Amalekite man.

The Amalekite's story was likely a lie, as the account of Saul's death from the writer of I Samuel says that Saul killed himself. It appears that the Amalekite man believed David wanted Saul to die, so he fabricated the story to impress him. He even provided the crown as evidence, assuming that he would be praised for his act. The irony is that in I Samuel 15, the Lord instructed Saul to destroy all of the Amalekites, and Saul was disobedient. Then in II Samuel 1, an Amalekite took credit for Saul's death. His sin eventually contributed to his demise.

REFLECTION: Just like Saul didn't completely kill the Amalekites, sometimes we are guilty of not completely killing our sin. We only partially obey what God tells us to do. We get comfortable within our sin and label it as "not that bad." The problem is, however, that the longer we allow sin to remain alive, the more at risk we are of it leading to our demise.

TODAY'S PRAYER: Father, make my heart sensitive to the Holy Spirit's convictions so that I might defeat sin. Amen.

The Murder of Ishbosheth

Read II Samuel 4

SUMMARY: In II Samuel 2, David was anointed as the new king of Judah, but Saul's son Ishbosheth was named king of the rest of Israel. One day, two men named Baanah and Rechab murdered Ishbosheth while he was sleeping. They cut off his head and presented it to David. David was upset by this, so he ordered his men to kill them.

Baanah and Rechab knew that Ishbosheth had not done anything wrong, and they knew that he wasn't really a threat to David's kingdom. While they made it seem like they were seeking justice for David and their cause was noble, they were really just seeking his approval and looking for a reward.

REFLECTION: Have you ever hidden ill intentions behind a facade of noble motives? Perhaps you treated someone poorly but claimed that it was okay because they had wronged you first. Or, maybe you took something that didn't belong to you, but justified it because the person who owned it didn't need it. We must be careful not to claim that something is acceptable when God's Word clearly speaks against it. It is never God's desire for us to do evil—especially when we try to hide it or justify it in his name. The more you attempt to justify your actions, the less likely you are to learn from your mistakes. The best course of action is to be honest with yourself, repent, and turn away from any wrongdoing.

TODAY'S PRAYER: Father, forgive me for the times that I have attempted to justify my sins instead of repenting. Amen.

Moving the Ark of the Covenant to Jerusalem

Read II Samuel 6:1-8

SUMMARY: David gathered 30,000 men to bring the Ark of the Covenant to Jerusalem. They placed the Ark of the Covenant on a cart and had two men guiding the cart as they moved. When they arrived at the threshing floor of Nacon, the oxen stumbled, and Uzzah reached out to steady the Ark. This angered the Lord, so He struck and killed Uzzah.

God had given Israel instructions for transporting the Ark of the Covenant. The Ark was to be carried on the shoulders of the priests, not transported on a cart. It is unclear as to why the Israelites did not follow God's instructions. It had been a while since the Israelites had the Ark of the Covenant in their possession, so they may have forgotten, but regardless, they did not obey God's law. Although the intentions of the Israelites were likely good, their lack of respect for God's direction was cause for punishment.

REFLECTION: Sometimes we have good intentions to do things that will bring glory to God, but we forget to seek God's direction first. We speak out on political matters without praying to God for clarity. We rebuke our brother or sister without reading the Bible to see what God's Word has to say about handling conflict. While we don't mean any harm, it is disrespectful to our all-knowing and all-powerful God. If God is truly at the head of our lives, then the way we handle situations should reflect that.

TODAY'S PRAYER: Father, forgive me for the times that I attempted to act without first seeking Your direction. Help me to walk in obedience to Your will. Amen.

Obed-edom

Read II Samuel 6:9-15

SUMMARY: David was afraid to bring the Ark of the Covenant back to Jerusalem, so he chose to take it to the house of Obed-edom. During that time, the Lord blessed Obed-edom and his family. When David found out about Obed-edom's favor, he retrieved the Ark of the Covenant and took it to Jerusalem.

David likely thought that leaving the Ark of the Covenant in Obed-edom's house would be a death sentence for Obed-edom and his family. Obed-edom, however, did not shy away from welcoming God's presence into his home. He and his family respected the Ark, and because of his commitment to his task, the Lord blessed him and his family.

REFLECTION: Sometimes, like the Israelites, we can be hesitant to accept an assignment when we have watched others fail at it. We may be scared to go to college because a family member dropped out. We may be scared to take a leadership position because we witnessed someone else being treated poorly in that role. But just because something didn't work for someone else doesn't mean that it won't work for you. If God has given you peace about a situation, then move forward in faith. When you accept challenges that others have avoided, you open yourself to blessings and divine breakthroughs that they may never experience.

TODAY'S PRAYER: Father, help me not to let fear block what You have for me. Give me clarity and peace as I follow Your will. Amen.

Michal's Contempt for David

Read II Samuel 6:16-23

SUMMARY: As the Ark of the Covenant entered the City of David, David danced before the Lord. Michal saw him dancing and became upset. She confronted David regarding what she saw as vulgar dancing, and as punishment, she never had a child of her own.

Michal was the daughter of King Saul and the first wife of King David. She loved David, but she did not share his love for God. What she judged as David showing off was actually an act of affection towards the Lord. Because of her lack of faith, she misunderstood his motives. David had survived battles, had survived Saul's attempted attacks, and had become king. Then he successfully brought the Ark of the Covenant back to Jerusalem. He understood what God had done in his life and made sure that his praise reflected that.

REFLECTION: Just like David, not everyone will understand your praise. They don't know what God means to you or what God has done for you. You may be judged or talked about. Some people may question your motives. The good thing is that the recipient of your praise understands and approves. God knows your heart and is pleased by your worship. Don't allow the "Michals" in your life to stop you from giving God the glory.

TODAY'S PRAYER: Father, today I reflect on how good You have been to me. I am forever grateful. I thank You for the ability to give You unrestricted praise. I will spend all of my days worshiping You. Amen.

David Wants to Build a Temple

Read II Samuel 7:1-17

SUMMARY: After King David brought the Ark of the Covenant back to Jerusalem, he wanted to build a temple to house it. The prophet Nathan initially agreed with David's idea, but then he heard from the Lord. The Lord told Nathan to tell David that He did not need a temple at that time.

David's intentions to build a temple were pure. God had been so good to David, and David wanted to do something good for Him. Even Nathan the prophet felt that the idea was reasonable, which is why he gave his blessing. The Lord, however, refused David's offer. It wasn't that it was bad, but it wasn't part of God's plan for David. Instead, He chose to bless David with a permanent house—a dynasty that would last forever.

REFLECTION: Sometimes we can have great plans that are outside of God's will. Our intentions can be pure, our reasoning can be appropriate, but they can still not match God's vision for our lives. This is why we have to be sensitive to the will of God and intentional about obedience. We have to be flexible with our plans and understand that He has the final say. God knows what is best for His kingdom, so we must remain open to His leadership. We have to trust that if our plans don't align, it is because He is bringing us to something better than we could have imagined.

TODAY'S PRAYER: Father, it can be hard to let go of my vision for my life when it doesn't align with Yours, but today I choose to surrender it to You. I trust that You know what is best for me and for Your kingdom. Use me as You see fit. Amen.

David's Kindness to Mephibosheth

Read II Samuel 9

SUMMARY: David was looking for a descendant of Saul to show kindness to because of his covenant with Jonathan. Saul's servant Ziba advised David that Jonathan's son, Mephibosheth, was still alive. David gave Mephibosheth everything that belonged to Saul and his family, including having Ziba and his sons as his servants. From that point on, Mephibosheth was invited to eat at David's table like one of David's own sons.

In II Samuel 4, it says that after Saul and Jonathan were killed in battle, Mephibosheth's nurse took him and ran away. She dropped him in the process, and he became crippled. Since that time, Mephibosheth had been hiding from David. He was afraid that David would try to kill him since, technically, he was an heir to the throne.

REFLECTION: Similar to Mephibosheth, some of us have been hiding as well. We are ashamed of the sin that has crippled us. We are fearful of being punished by God for our past. But like David, it is not God's desire to condemn us, but rather to meet us in love. He desires a relationship with us. He wants us to sit at His table and fellowship with Him. So, will you be like Mephibosheth and accept God's invitation? If you haven't already, choose to accept God's offer of unmerited love and favor today.

TODAY'S PRAYER: Father, when I was hiding from You because of my guilt and sin, You found me. Thank You for caring about me in the middle of my mess. Amen.

David and Bathsheba

Read II Samuel 11

SUMMARY: King David committed adultery with a woman named Bathsheba, and then she became pregnant. To hide the paternity of the baby, David called her husband, Uriah, away from battle so that he could sleep with his wife. Uriah was empathetic to the men who were in battle while he was at home, so he refused to sleep with her. David then sent him to the frontline of battle to kill him, and then he took Bathsheba to be his wife. What began as temptation escalated into greater sin.

REFLECTION: When we reflect on moments of sin in our lives, we often realize there were opportunities to avoid them. The first way to guard against sin is to remain watchful. Stay in God's Word and stay close to Him so you can discern the enemy's schemes. Second, make sure you are where you are supposed to be, doing what God has called you to do. David should have been leading his army, but instead, he stayed home. Had he been with his men, he never would have seen Bathsheba. Third, consider the consequences of sin. Are we truly willing to risk everything for a fleeting moment of pleasure? God always provides a way out—our responsibility is to choose it.

TODAY'S PRAYER: Father, dealing with temptation is never easy, so I am leaning on You for help. I ask that You give me the wisdom to be mindful of situations that could lead me into temptation. Give me the strength to walk away. Amen.

Nathan Rebukes David

Read II Samuel 12:1-14

SUMMARY: The prophet Nathan came to David and told him a story about a man who was rich but took the only possession that a poor man had and killed it for his guests. David was angered by this story until he realized that the story was about him. Nathan told David that, as punishment for his actions against Uriah, his household would be stricken by violence and rebel against him. Nathan also told David that his son would die. Even though God forgave David for his sins, there were still consequences for his actions.

REFLECTION: As Christians, we have to accept the fact that there can be consequences associated with sin, even after we repent. It doesn't mean that God doesn't love us, and it doesn't mean that we aren't forgiven. We are still saved by grace, but we also have to take responsibility for what has been done and how it has affected others. Like David, in those moments we shouldn't be mad at God or question our relationship with Him, but we should rather accept the repercussions of our actions in humility.

TODAY'S PRAYER: Father, I thank You for forgiving me when I have done wrong. I ask that You give me wisdom and strength to avoid temptation. When I do sin, help me to return to You with a repentant heart. Amen.

The Death of David's Son

Read II Samuel 12:15-25

SUMMARY: The Lord caused David's son to have a deadly illness. David begged God to spare his son. He stopped eating and lay on the ground all night, refusing to get up. After seven days, David's son died. His advisors were hesitant to tell him, but when David found out, he got up, cleaned himself, worshiped the Lord, and then ate. He comforted his wife, Bathsheba. She soon became pregnant again and gave birth to a son named Solomon.

How could David be at peace with his son's death when he reacted so poorly to the news of his son's illness? David's response explained his actions. He had begged God to allow his child to live, and God had answered. There was nothing more that he could do, and he respected God's decision.

REFLECTION: While it is perfectly normal to mourn the loss of a loved one, David's actions show us how to respond when God denies our requests. He gives us a playbook as to how to react when God says "no" to what we thought was a part of His plan. We can pray, fast, and cry out to Him—but when His answer is final, our role is to trust His will. True faith finds peace not in the outcome we wanted, but in confidence that God knows what is best.

TODAY'S PRAYER: Father, I acknowledge that sometimes I get upset when You tell me "no," but I know that Your plan is what is best for me. Help me to find peace in Your decision. Amen.

Tamar and Amnon

Read II Samuel 13

SUMMARY: Amnon and Tamar were half-siblings through their father, David. Amnon fell "in love" with Tamar to the point where he became sick because he couldn't have her. Amnon's friend came up with a plan for him to be alone with Tamar. It was then that Amnon raped her. Two years later, Tamar's brother Absalom murdered Amnon.

So much of what we do is influenced by the opinions of others. When we want to do wrong, it is often easy to find someone who will affirm our thinking. Agreement can make sin feel justified. This was the case with Amnon. He knew his desire for his sister was wrong—that is why it made him sick. But once his friend normalized his thoughts, Amnon began to believe that what was sinful was acceptable.

REFLECTION: We have to be careful to discern the difference between good and bad counsel, especially when we are experiencing temptation. It's not enough to just listen to what sounds good at the moment. We truly need to process the advice and make sure that it is sound. Don't be afraid to ask God for wisdom. He knows all, and that includes the hearts of those around you. If the advice of your counsel doesn't align with that of God, you will know that they aren't worth listening to.

TODAY'S PRAYER: Father, I am constantly surrounded by many choices and even more opinions. Please give me discernment as I seek godly counsel. I pray that You will guide the people in my life who will provide me with wisdom and spiritual leadership. Amen.

The Wise Woman of Tekoa

Read II Samuel 14:1-24

SUMMARY: There was a woman from the town of Tekoa in Judah who was known for her wisdom. Joab had her dress up in mourning clothes and fabricate a story to share with King David. The story was similar to the king's own life, in which his son Absalom had murdered his other son Amnon. In this way, the woman of Tekoa was able to convince the king to bring Absalom back to Jerusalem. She showed him that by refusing to show mercy to his own son, he was doing more harm than good.

REFLECTION: Has someone ever hurt you to the point that you removed them from your life? Is there a family member or friend who you previously alienated, but now you are reconsidering things? Forgiveness is necessary, but reconciliation looks different in every situation. Some relationships are too harmful to restore, and it is okay to leave them in the past.

Other times, distance causes more pain than healing. Some relationships are worth restoring. If you feel a desire to reconnect with someone, pray for clarity. Ask God to guide your perspective and your steps. Trust Him to lead you toward restoration, according to His will.

TODAY'S PRAYER: Father, give me wisdom and clarity concerning relationships that need healing. Help me to trust Your guidance in every situation. Amen.

Absalom's Rebellion

Read II Samuel 15

SUMMARY: Absalom won the hearts of the people by appearing helpful and compassionate, but his true goal was to seize the throne. He spread doubt about David's leadership and portrayed the king as indifferent to the people's needs. When David learned of Absalom's plan, he fled Jerusalem and sent Hushai back to counter the counsel of Ahithophel, who had joined Absalom.

Absalom's charm, appearance, and words deceived the people. By exaggerating problems and questioning David's care and competence, he caused the Israelites to mistrust the king God had anointed.

REFLECTION: We must be cautious of people like Absalom who appear caring but have selfish motives. Those who stir conflict, sow doubt, and rebel against God's authority can lead us away from truth. The "Absaloms" of the world are not our friends. They simply desire to use us, and if we aren't careful, they could turn us away from God.

Let us be prayerful that the Lord would reveal to us the true intentions of the people around us. Let us exercise discernment so that we aren't easily moved by their emotional rhetoric. Let us seek wise counsel before we turn our allegiance away from the people that we once trusted.

TODAY'S PRAYER: Father, open my eyes to the true intentions of those around me. Give me discernment and protect me from deception. Amen.

The Wise Woman of Abel-Beth-Maacah

Read II Samuel 20

SUMMARY: There was a man named Sheba who was from the tribe of Benjamin. He encouraged the men of Israel to rebel against David and follow him instead. All of the men of Israel, except those from the tribe of Judah, did so. Abishai and Joab chased after Sheba and ended up in the town of Abel-Beth-Maacah. They were preparing to destroy the wall around the town, but a wise woman asked to speak with Joab. She agreed to give Joab the head of Sheba in exchange for the troops to leave.

One thing that we can learn from the woman in this story is how to handle conflict. The wise woman saw Joab preparing to destroy the town, and she calmly spoke out. She didn't call Joab names or insult his intelligence. She reasoned with him and learned that he only wanted to kill one person. She strategized with her people and came up with terms that were agreeable to both parties.

REFLECTION: How do you respond to conflict—emotionally, passively, or wisely? Let us learn from the wise woman that it is possible to get your point across without tearing someone down. It is possible to successfully compromise with others. Let us handle conflict with wisdom, self-control, and confidence.

TODAY'S PRAYER: Father, give me wisdom and confidence to handle conflict well. Help me to speak calmly and act wisely, even in difficult situations. Amen.

Rizpah Mourns

Read II Samuel 21:1-14

SUMMARY: During David's reign, there was a three-year famine. It occurred because Saul had murdered the Gibeonites, a group of people that the Israelites had sworn against killing. The Gibeonites told David that to rectify the situation, they wanted seven of Saul's sons to be handed over to them for execution. Two of the men chosen were Saul's sons by a woman named Rizpah. After the execution, Rizpah stayed on the mountain, protecting the bodies from wild animals. When David learned of her actions, he ensured a proper burial for all the men, and then God ended the famine.

Though Rizpah seemed powerless, her quiet perseverance moved the king's heart. The famine ended not just because justice was carried out, but because compassion was shown.

REFLECTION: Whether it's because of your race, gender, age, social status, or even a disability, there will come a time when you feel powerless. There will be a moment when you feel like you can't make a difference in your life or the lives of others. During that time, remember Rizpah. She was a concubine and a woman, yet in her silent protest, she was able to make a difference. Know that regardless of who you are, you can create change. Your voice, your opinion, and your feelings matter. Don't be afraid to stand up for what you believe in.

TODAY'S PRAYER: Father, I know that You have a purpose and a plan for me. Whether big or small, I thank You for showing me that I can make a difference in this world. Amen.

David Takes a Census

Read II Samuel 24

SUMMARY: David ordered a census of all the tribes of Israel despite Joab's warning that it would be a sin against the Lord. Afterward, David felt guilty and repented. God allowed David to choose his punishment, and he chose a three-day plague. God sent an angel to destroy Jerusalem, but He stopped the angel just as it was about to destroy the city. David saw the angel with its sword drawn and repented again. He built an altar to the Lord and sacrificed offerings.

In those times, a census was done to determine the size of a potential army. That way, if conflict arose, one would know how many men were available to fight. The problem was that David was supposed to be trusting in the Lord. It shouldn't have mattered how many men he had if his faith was strong.

REFLECTION: How often are we like David, saying that we trust in the Lord, but in reality only trusting in what we can see? How many times have we leaned on our own understanding instead of surrendering to the power of God? May we always be mindful that God doesn't need us to perform His works. The size of an army doesn't matter when God is in control, and neither do our own strength and abilities. If we say that we trust God, let us demonstrate it with our actions.

TODAY'S PRAYER: Father, forgive me for the times when I claimed to trust You, but my actions did not reflect it. I pray for continued grace on my journey of trusting You with my whole heart. Amen.

Adonijah Claims the Throne

Read I Kings 1:5-53

SUMMARY: David was becoming older, and his son Adonijah began telling people that he planned to make himself king. Nathan the prophet heard of Adonijah's plans and reported them to Solomon's mother, Bathsheba. Through Bathsheba, word got back to David, who immediately called for Solomon to be anointed king over Israel. When Adonijah's supporters heard that Solomon was the new king, they abandoned him out of fear.

Adonijah was prideful and selfish. He saw his father's weak state as an opportunity to be exalted. Scripture notes that David never disciplined him, implying that Adonijah's character flaws were rooted in a lack of correction. This story highlights the consequences of no discipline and the role correction plays in shaping character.

REFLECTION: Were you disciplined as a child? How did that mold you into the person you are today? Believe it or not, discipline, when done right, is a reflection of love. You teach children to do right because you want them to grow up to be responsible adults. You correct children when they do wrong so that they don't have to face the consequences of poor decisions in the future. Just as God lovingly disciplines us, we are called to guide the next generation with wisdom and care.

TODAY'S PRAYER: Father, give me wisdom to discipline with love and clarity. Help those I correct to see my heart and Your purpose through it. Amen.

Gifts for Building the Temple

Read I Chronicles 28:1-29:9

SUMMARY: David brought together the officials of Israel and presented Solomon as their next king. He tasked Solomon with building a temple for the Lord. David gave Solomon detailed plans and the resources to begin building. When the leaders saw how much David contributed to the temple, they also gave of what they had.

David understood that it was not God's plan for him to build the Lord's Temple, so he took what he had and used it to help Solomon. He brought gold and silver, and the plans for the courtyards and the rooms. He ensured that Solomon would be successful in doing what he was unable to do.

REFLECTION: This story reminds us that even when we are not called to complete a task ourselves, we can still play a vital role in God's work. Sometimes our purpose is simply to prepare the way for others. Faithfulness isn't only found in what we build, but also in how we help others build what God has placed on their hearts.

Take time this week to identify someone you can support—through encouragement, mentorship, prayer, or resources. Ask God how you can use what He has given you to help someone else succeed.

TODAY'S PRAYER: Father, help me to trust You when my plans change. Show me how to use what I have to encourage and support others. Amen.

Solomon Asks for Wisdom

Read I Kings 3

SUMMARY: The Lord appeared to Solomon in a dream and told him that He would give him whatever he desired. Solomon asked the Lord for wisdom. The Lord was pleased, so He gave Solomon wisdom but also blessed him with fame and riches.

Solomon's wisdom was demonstrated when two women came to him claiming the same baby. Solomon called for a sword and commanded that the living child be cut in half so that each woman could have a portion of him. One woman wanted the baby to live, while the other woman was fine with the command. Solomon then declared that the child should be given to the woman who wanted him to live, as she was clearly the real mother.

REFLECTION: Perhaps you have a tough time making decisions. It can be overwhelming when one choice could have important or lasting effects. The good thing is that God already knows the future and invites us to seek His wisdom. Trust Him to guide your decision-making and to redirect you when needed. God loves you and will always lead you well.

TODAY'S PRAYER: Father, sometimes making decisions can be scary. The fear that a wrong choice could negatively affect the people in my life adds a lot of pressure. I ask that You give me wisdom to make sound decisions, just like You did for Solomon. Guide my thoughts and lead me on the right path. Amen.

Solomon's Many Wives

Read I Kings 11:1-13

SUMMARY: Solomon had 700 wives and 300 concubines of various nationalities. When Solomon became old, the women influenced him to worship idols. He built shrines for all of his foreign wives to use for sacrificing to their gods. The Lord was angry with Solomon and promised to take the kingdom away from Solomon's son. Solomon's son was only allowed to be king of one tribe because of the Lord's promise to David.

In Solomon's early years, the Lord gave him wisdom, but it seems that as he got older, he chose to do what he wanted to do. Solomon was concerned about his success as king. By marrying foreign women, he was able to make political alliances that would benefit him. Although the Lord had warned all of the Israelites that marrying foreign women would lead to idolatry, Solomon likely felt that he was too wise and powerful to be swayed.

REFLECTION: As believers, we can mistakenly think we are above temptation, but no one is immune to sin. Even with the full armor of God, we should be careful about the decisions that we make and the environments that we place ourselves in. We are still human and capable of making mistakes. The only way to avoid sin is to be humble and obedient to God.

TODAY'S PRAYER: Father, help me to rely on You instead of my own understanding. Teach me to walk in obedience and humility. Amen.

Rehoboam Seeks Advice

Read I Kings 12:1-24

SUMMARY: Rehoboam was the son of Solomon. When it was time for him to become king, the leaders of Israel asked him to lighten the labor demands and lessen the taxes that Solomon had put on them. Rehoboam asked for three days to consider their request. Rehoboam discussed the situation with some older men, and they advised him to do as the leaders had requested. Rehoboam ignored their advice and chose to listen to some younger men who told him to be even harsher than Solomon. As a result, the northern tribes of Israel refused to be ruled by him.

Even before he was officially king, Rehoboam had an important decision to make. While he was right to take his time and seek advice from others, he didn't trust the right people. In the end, he made a bad decision that produced bad results.

REFLECTION: Who do you go to for advice—a family member, a friend, a pastor? Choosing wise counsel matters. Seek out people who demonstrate godly character and genuinely have your best interest at heart. It would also be wise to find someone who has successfully handled a similar situation and can lead you in the right direction. Above all, you should seek wisdom from God. Pray for clarity and direction. God knows all, sees all, and wants you to prosper.

TODAY'S PRAYER: Father, I ask that You protect me from the influence of people who could lead me to make poor decisions. Help me to seek and follow Your wisdom. Amen.

Jeroboam's Golden Calves

Read I Kings 12:25-13:10

SUMMARY: The ten northern tribes of Israel refused to accept Solomon's son Rehoboam as king, so they chose Jeroboam to be their king. King Jeroboam worried that the Israelites would give their allegiance back to King Rehoboam if they traveled to Jerusalem to offer sacrifices, so he created two golden calves for the people to worship within the borders of his kingdom. By making worship convenient and familiar, he led the Israelites into idol worship. God sent a prophet to warn Jeroboam that a future king, Josiah from David's lineage, would one day destroy the altar he built.

REFLECTION: Jeroboam made worship easy, comfortable, and appealing —but it was no longer centered on God. It raises an important question: has our worship become about convenience rather than glorifying Him? Too often, we choose worship that fits our schedules, avoids conviction, and asks little of us. True worship is not about what we receive but what we offer to God. When our hearts are focused on honoring Him, worship becomes an act of gratitude rather than convenience.

Take time today to evaluate your worship. Ask God to reveal any areas where convenience has replaced devotion.

TODAY'S PRAYER: Father, forgive me for the times that I chose my convenience over true worship. Today, I commit to putting You first and worshiping You in spirit and in truth. Amen.

The Deceptive Prophet

Read I Kings 13:11-34

SUMMARY: As the prophet was heading home after rebuking Jeroboam, he met an older prophet who invited him to his house to eat. The prophet declined because the Lord had told him not to eat or drink anything while on his journey. The older prophet falsely claimed that an angel had instructed him to take the younger prophet home and feed him. The younger prophet believed him and followed him home. While they were sitting, the Lord spoke through the older prophet and told the younger prophet that he would be punished for disobeying God's instructions. As the younger prophet headed home, a lion came out and killed him.

The young prophet was sensitive to the Lord's voice when he spoke to Jeroboam, but it seems as if he let his guard down once he left. He trusted a man's word over God's clear instructions.

REFLECTION: Like the young prophet, we may encounter people who claim to speak for God but have not truly been sent by Him. If we are not careful, their words can lead us away from God's will. We have to be mindful to test every spirit and use discernment. Ask yourself this: Does the word they were given align with Scripture and with what God has been telling you? Pray and ask God for confirmation before you act. The devil wants nothing more than for us to believe his lies, so we must always be on guard.

TODAY'S PRAYER: Father, protect me from the plans of the enemy. Give me discernment to recognize Your voice and reject anything that does not come from You. Amen.

The Prophecy Against Jeroboam

Read I Kings 14:1-20

SUMMARY: Jeroboam's son became sick, so his wife disguised herself and went to the prophet Ahijah for guidance. The prophet told Jeroboam's wife that because of Jeroboam's sin, the Lord was going to end his dynasty. He also told her that once she returned to her city, her son would die, and eventually, Israel would be exiled from the Promised Land.

There are likely many reasons why Jeroboam had his wife disguise herself to see the prophet. He could have been ashamed of how he had turned away from God, or it's possible that he didn't want the rest of the Israelites to know that he was turning back to God in his moment of need. Whatever the case, as soon as Jeroboam's wife entered Ahijah's home, God revealed to Ahijah exactly who she was.

REFLECTION: Like Jeroboam's wife, we sometimes approach God wearing a disguise—hiding our true feelings, fears, or desires out of shame. But, in reality, we can never hide from God. He sees everything, even those things that you have successfully hidden from others. God is our father, and He wants us to approach Him openly. Step out of the shadows and into the light by bringing your whole heart before Him.

TODAY'S PRAYER: Father, You know all about me. I can never escape Your presence. Give me the courage to share with You my flaws, needs, and desires. Amen.

Elijah is Fed by Ravens

Read I Kings 17:1-7

SUMMARY: Elijah told King Ahab that there would be a drought for the next few years. Then he ran and hid by a brook where he could drink water. The Lord sent ravens to bring him food.

While this story is fairly short, it highlights the obedience of the prophet Elijah. Elijah had to tell a notoriously evil king bad news. The task was dangerous, but he didn't hesitate to follow God's instructions. Because of Elijah's obedience, God gave him a place of protection and a means to get food and water.

REFLECTION: Is there something that God has been telling you to do but you haven't done it yet? Perhaps God wants you to write a book or start a business. Maybe God wants you to leave a toxic relationship. Perhaps God just wants you to get back in church. Learn from Elijah's obedience. You may find that, like Elijah, your obedience is tied to God's provision. The task may not be easy; it may even feel dangerous, but we can trust that He will give us what we need each step of the way.

TODAY'S PRAYER: Father, help me to be obedient to You even when I am afraid. Give me peace knowing that You are with me. Amen.

The Widow at Zarephath

Read I Kings 17:8-24

SUMMARY: The Lord told Elijah to go to the village of Zarephath, as He had instructed a widow to feed him there. When Elijah approached the widow and asked for food, the widow told him that she only had enough flour and oil for one final meal for herself and her son. Though hesitant, she obeyed, and God miraculously ensured that her flour and oil never ran out.

REFLECTION: Have you ever received a word from God, but your circumstances didn't match His promise? For example, maybe God promised you that you would have a new home this year, but you just lost your job. Or maybe God promised you health, but you just got a bad report from the doctor. In those moments, faith can feel uncertain and confusing. Yet obedience often requires trust before understanding. Elijah didn't walk away after the widow declined his first request. He didn't question if he heard God correctly. He persisted in faith.

At times, hearing from God can be difficult and confusing, but don't give up. Continue in faith. Trust that God has a plan, and be present for the miracle He is preparing.

TODAY'S PRAYER: Father, I am grateful that You always have a plan for me and that Your intentions for me are good. Help me to trust You even when I don't understand what is going on. Lead me and direct me in the way that I should go. Amen.

The Contest on Mount Carmel

Read I Kings 18:1-40

SUMMARY: After hiding for more than 3 years, the Lord instructed Elijah to reveal himself to King Ahab. Elijah challenged the prophets of Baal and Asherah to a contest to determine who the real God was. The prophets of Baal prepared a sacrifice and chanted and danced, but there was no response from Baal. Then Elijah called the people over to the altar of the Lord. He prepared a sacrifice and then poured water over the offering and wood three times. Elijah prayed, and the Lord sent fire down to burn the offering. When the people saw this, they acknowledged that the Lord was the true God.

REFLECTION: While we don't have to deal with the prophets of Baal anymore, we still deal with all sorts of idols that try to pull us away from serving the one true God. Like Elijah, it may feel like we're all alone when we choose to live for God. It can be difficult as a Christian to watch your loved ones enjoying the sinful pleasures of the world. You may feel isolated when you tell your family or friends that you can't take part in the things you used to do before you decided to follow Christ. But, just like in the story, the reality is that we are not alone. Even in moments where we aren't able to fellowship with believers, we must always remember that God is with us. When we call on Him in prayer, He will show up and provide us with what we need.

TODAY'S PRAYER: Father, I thank You for always listening to and answering my prayers. I am never alone because You are always with me. Amen.

Elijah Prays for Rain

Read I Kings 18:41-46

SUMMARY: After the prophets of Baal were killed, King Ahab went to eat, and Elijah went to pray. Elijah then told his servant to look out towards the sea. Six times, the servant looked and saw nothing, but the seventh time he saw a small cloud. Elijah's prophecy was coming to pass. As the rain started falling, King Ahab left for Jezreel. The power of the Lord came upon Elijah, and he took off running faster than King Ahab in his chariot.

The Bible says that Elijah told the king that rain was coming and instructed King Ahab to eat. For probably the first time, King Ahab obeyed him. King Ahab was not a fan of Elijah, but after witnessing what happened on Mt. Carmel, he knew the power that the God of Elijah had. Even without a dark cloud in the sky, he ate with confidence that the rain was coming.

REFLECTION: As believers, through reading the Bible, through the testimonies of others, and through our own experiences, we know who God is and what He can do. Therefore, when God instructs us to do something, we should act in obedience. Like King Ahab, we shouldn't need a sign of what is to come before we act. We can move in confidence simply because God said it.

TODAY'S PRAYER: Father, I know that all things are possible in You. I ask that You strengthen my faith as I continue to pursue obedience. Amen.

Elijah Flees to Sinai

Read I Kings 19:1-18

SUMMARY: Jezebel threatened to kill Elijah, so he fled to the wilderness. He was exhausted and prayed that the Lord would take his life. As he was sleeping, an angel woke him up and made him eat so that he could have strength for his journey. Later, the Lord came to him and spoke to him in a gentle whisper. He instructed Elijah to anoint a new king of Aram, a new king of Israel, and a new prophet.

Elijah was exhibiting signs of depression. He was fearful because of Jezebel's threats. He felt incompetent because, despite his efforts, Israel was continuing to worship idols. Elijah was burnt out because he was the only prophet of God left. He wasn't concerned about eating, and he wanted to die. But in the midst of Elijah's depression, God showed him that He cared. He provided him with food and water, He gave Elijah time to rest, and He made His presence known with a "still small voice."

REFLECTION: Even strong believers experience seasons of weariness and doubt. There may be some tough days, weeks, months, or even years when life feels heavy and purpose seems unclear, but God still cares deeply. He is near, listening, and present—even in silence. In seasons like these, rest is often one of the ways God begins His work of restoration. Trust that God will renew your strength when the time is right and guide you forward.

TODAY'S PRAYER: Father, thank You for being with me in my lowest moments. Help me to recognize when I need rest and give me the strength to ask for help. Amen.

The Call of Elisha

Read I Kings 19:19-21

SUMMARY: God had instructed Elijah to anoint Elisha to replace him as God's prophet. When Elijah came to Elisha, Elisha was plowing a field. After Elijah threw his cloak across Elisha's shoulders, Elisha slaughtered the oxen that he was using to plow the field and fed the townspeople. Then he followed Elijah and became his assistant.

Elisha knew of the dangers that Elijah had faced. He knew that his new assignment would not always be enjoyable, but he decided to fully accept God's plan. The oxen were essential to Elisha's previous livelihood. He couldn't plow the fields efficiently without them. So by slaughtering them, he was making a point. There was no turning back.

REFLECTION: Every Christian has been called to do something that requires courage and complete trust in God. Take notes from Elisha and choose God's plans over your own interests. Be unwavering in your devotedness to Him. Trust that when you put God's plans first, He will honor your desires.

TODAY'S PRAYER: Father, I ask for the courage to deny myself and be wholly devoted to You. I accept Your plan for my life, even if I don't fully know what that entails. Amen.

Naboth's Vineyard

Read I Kings 21

SUMMARY: King Ahab wanted to acquire Naboth's vineyard near his palace to turn it into a vegetable garden. He offered to buy it or exchange it for a better vineyard, but Naboth refused because it was his inheritance. Angered, Ahab complained, and his wife Jezebel devised a scheme to seize the land. She orchestrated false accusations against Naboth, leading to his death by stoning. God declared that Ahab's dynasty would face judgment and that Jezebel would meet a humiliating death. Though Ahab repented, full judgment came after his death.

REFLECTION: Have you ever heard of the "Jezebel spirit?" The "Jezebel spirit" refers to a person who has a spirit that seeks to dominate others and promote sin. Jezebel used influence, intimidation, and deception to achieve her desires, leaving a trail of destruction in the process.

This spirit is not only a thing of the past; it can appear in workplaces, families, communities, and even within ourselves—anywhere ambition, manipulation, or deceit overrides God's will. Jezebel's story warns us to be vigilant: we must discern when someone's influence seeks to lead us away from righteousness and guard our hearts against adopting similar attitudes.

TODAY'S PRAYER: Father, protect me from the influence of manipulation, control, and deceit. Expose any "Jezebel spirit" at work around me or within me, and give me courage to stand firm in truth. Amen.

Micaiah the Prophet

Read I Kings 22:1-40

SUMMARY: King Ahab asked King Jehoshaphat to join him in battle. King Jehoshaphat agreed to the plan, but he wanted to seek the Lord's advice first. They asked 400 false prophets if they should go to war, and each one of them encouraged them to do so. Finally, they found a prophet of the Lord named Micaiah. He prophesied that there would be trouble if they went to war. They threw Micaiah into prison and went into battle despite his warning. King Ahab decided to disguise himself so that he would not be recognized, but was killed by a stray arrow.

Initially, it seems noble that the kings thought to seek the Lord's advice, but when you dig further into the text, it seems like they were only willing to accept one answer. When Micaiah finally told them the truth, they punished him for his honesty and continued to do what they wanted to do.

REFLECTION: How often do we ask God for guidance but reject His answer when it doesn't align with what we want? Instead of trusting Him, we lean on our own understanding and later regret it.

Is there something that you have been asking God for clarity about? Make sure that you are prepared for His answer. May we all learn to trust God and take heed to His instruction.

TODAY'S PRAYER: Father, help me not only to seek Your will but to obey it. Amen.

Elijah Confronts King Ahaziah

Read II Kings 1

SUMMARY: King Ahaziah was the new king of Israel. One day, he fell through the floor of an upper room of his palace and was seriously injured. He sent messengers to inquire of Baalzebub, the god of Ekron, to see whether he would recover. An angel told Elijah to confront the king's messengers and tell them that because King Ahaziah went to an idol god instead of the Lord, he would die. Just as Elijah promised, the king died, and his brother became the next king.

King Ahaziah had absolutely no faith, and he didn't even try to pretend as if he did. He obviously knew who Elijah was and what he did because he identified him based on the description of his messengers. When he was injured, he could have personally prayed to God for healing or sought out God's prophet, but instead, he sent his men to the temple of an idol god. Even when he received the message that he would die, he chose to act in anger instead of humbling himself and repenting.

REFLECTION: When trouble comes, who do you turn to first—family, friends, or God? Our God is Sovereign, meaning that He is the only ruler. We shouldn't put anyone before Him. He has proven to be a help in times of trouble. He deserves our trust and our obedience.

TODAY'S PRAYER: Father, increase my faith so that when troubles come, I can have peace in leaning on You. Amen.

Elijah is Taken into Heaven

Read II Kings 2:1-18

SUMMARY: Before Elijah was taken up into Heaven, he asked Elisha what he could do for him. Elisha didn't ask for any material things, but instead he requested a double portion of God's spirit and to become Elijah's successor.

In biblical times, a double portion was the amount of property and earnings that a father would pass down to his son. Elijah wasn't Elisha's biological father, but he did play the role of a spiritual father to him. So, in reality, his request was appropriate. Elijah told Elisha that he was asking for a lot, but in the end, God granted Elisha's request.

REFLECTION: There is no such thing as asking for too much when it comes to wanting more of God. Elisha did not ask for wealth, status, or comfort—he asked for a deeper measure of God's Spirit so he could faithfully carry on the work he had been called to do. His request reveals a heart that valued spiritual inheritance over material gain.

Like Elisha, we are invited to examine what we truly desire from God. Do we seek His presence, power, and guidance, or are we more focused on what He can give us? God honors a heart that longs to know Him more and to walk in His purposes.

TODAY'S PRAYER: Father, I desire to grow closer to You every day. Today, I ask that You give me a heart for You and Your Word. Amen.

Elisha is Teased by Children

Read II Kings 2:23-25

SUMMARY: As Elisha was walking, a group of boys made fun of his bald head. He cursed them in the name of the Lord, and two bears came and attacked forty-two of them.

REFLECTION: Have you ever read anything in the Bible that was hard to accept? We often think of God as gracious, merciful, and kind, yet stories like this can feel harsh and unsettling.

At the end of the day, the scripture says that God's ways are not our ways. He will do things that don't make sense to us, but we will still have to accept them. He is the only God. We must trust that even when we don't understand, He knows what is best.

TODAY'S PRAYER: Father, I see You as a loving God, but sometimes I don't always understand Your ways. In those moments, help me to recognize that there may be a bigger purpose. You see all and You know all, so I choose to trust in You. Amen.

War Against Moab

Read II Kings 3

SUMMARY: The King of Moab rebelled against Israel, so King Joram (Ahab's son) asked King Jehoshaphat of Judah and the king of Edom to join him in attacking the Moabites. After traveling in the wilderness to attack Moab, they realized that there was no water for them, so they consulted Elisha. Elisha prophesied that the Lord would fill the dry valley with water and give them victory over the Moabite army. The next day, water appeared, and the three armies defeated the Moabites.

Depending on which version of the story you read, Elisha's prophecy also came with instructions. In the King James Version of II Kings 3:16, it says, "Thus saith the Lord, Make this valley full of ditches." Before the army could receive the water, they had to dig ditches in the dry ground. Essentially, the people had to prepare themselves before they could receive their blessing.

REFLECTION: If you expect to receive God's blessing, you must prepare for it. Faith isn't passive; it acts in expectation. If you desire a home, you should know how to take care of it. If you desire a car, you first need to get your license. What would be the point of God blessing you if you aren't ready to receive it? Therefore, prepare your heart, your habits, and your life for what you believe God will do.

TODAY'S PRAYER: Father, I expect You to be true to Your Word. Help me to anticipate Your blessings by preparing myself to receive them. Amen.

Elisha Helps a Poor Widow

Read II Kings 4:1-7

SUMMARY: One day, a widow came to Elisha and told him that creditors were threatening to enslave her sons due to her debt. Elisha asked what she had in her home, and she replied that she only had a small jar of oil. He instructed her to borrow empty jars and pour the oil into them. As she obeyed, the oil continued to flow until every jar was filled. She sold the oil, paid her debts, and supported her family.

There's an old saying that goes "Give a man a fish, and you feed him for a day. Teach him how to fish, and you feed him for a lifetime." This story is a great example of how to put that proverb into action. Elisha could have given her money to solve her debt situation, but that would have only helped temporarily. Eventually, she would have likely found herself begging again. Instead, Elisha taught her how God could multiply what she already had.

REFLECTION: Sometimes the solution to our problems is already in our hands. God has placed gifts, talents, and resources within you that He desires to use. Don't allow fear or doubt to hold you back. When you offer what you have to God, He can multiply it beyond what you imagine.

TODAY'S PRAYER: Father, help me to recognize what You have already placed in my hands. Teach me to trust You as I step out in obedience, believing that You can multiply what I have for Your glory and my good. Amen.

Elisha and the Shunammite Woman

Read II Kings 4:8-37

SUMMARY: There was a wealthy woman in the town of Shunem who regularly welcomed Elisha into her home. Elisha wanted to do something kind for the woman, and his servant told him that she didn't have a son. Elisha prophesied that the next year she would have a son, and sure enough, it happened.

Several years later, the child suddenly died. The woman sought out Elisha, and he returned with her to the house. Elisha prayed earnestly to the Lord and stretched himself over the child twice. God restored the boy's life, and he was brought back to his mother.

When Elisha told the Shunammite woman that she would have a son by the next year, her response was basically "don't get my hopes up." The Shunammite woman had an unspoken desire, a dream that she had given up on due to life's circumstances. She had become content with the fact that it might never occur, so all was well with her. The beautiful thing is that God knows all. He knew about her unspoken desire and rewarded her with it because of her generosity.

REFLECTION: God knows your deepest desires, even the ones that you have given up on. The same God who gave the Shunammite woman her unspoken desire is still in the blessing business. What's uncommon to man is never too hard for God. Continue to be a blessing for others and watch God work on your behalf.

TODAY'S PRAYER: Father, thank You for blessing me in so many ways. Help me to give freely so that I may be a blessing to others. Amen.

Elisha Feeds 100

Read II Kings 4:42-44

SUMMARY: Elisha made his way to Gilgal in the middle of a famine. Elisha was given twenty loaves of bread made from the first grains of the harvest. Elisha instructed his servant to take the bread and feed 100 prophets. The Bible reports that all of the prophets had enough to eat, and there was still bread left over.

In moments of lack, it can be easy to allow fear to make us selfish and ignore the needs of others. Elisha, however, heard God say that there would be enough food for everyone. He didn't take the bread just for himself. He trusted God with the little and watched as the provision multiplied.

REFLECTION: How do you respond when God asks you to help others in moments when you're lacking? Do you hoard for yourself in doubt, or do you step out on faith and share with those in need? Over and over again, God reminds us that we can trust Him to provide even with our little. You'll never lack when you choose to help those in need.

TODAY'S PRAYER: Father, I thank You for taking what little I have and using it for Your glory. Amen.

Naaman's Healing

Read II Kings 5:1-19

SUMMARY: Naaman was the commander of the king's army, but he had leprosy. One day, a young maid suggested that Naaman see the prophet Elisha to be healed. Naaman didn't agree with Elisha's manner of healing him, but once he obeyed, he was healed of his leprosy.

Many times when we go through trials and tribulations, we have an idea of how God is going to help us, but what happens when our expectations don't match up with God's plan? Naaman had a set idea of how he would receive his healing. As a wealthy and successful person, it was likely offensive that Elisha would not even come to greet him and heal him in person. Naaman almost allowed pride to get in the way of his healing. Thankfully, he had people in his circle who encouraged him to humble himself and be obedient.

REFLECTION: It is important that we make sure that our inner circle has our best interests at heart. We need people who will challenge us and offer sound advice when it's needed. We need people who won't just tell us what we want to hear. We also have to be receptive to advice like Naaman was and not take offense.

Think about the individuals in your circle. Do they want the best for you? If so, are you willing to listen to them?

TODAY'S PRAYER: Father, please place people in my life who I can trust to give me the advice I need and not just the advice I want. I ask that You help me to be receptive to what they have to say. Amen.

Gehazi's Greed

Read II Kings 5:20-27

SUMMARY: Elisha refused to accept gifts from Naaman, but his servant, Gehazi, secretly took silver and clothing for himself. Gehazi thought Elisha wouldn't know about the deception, but the Lord revealed it to him. As punishment for lying, God gave Gehazi and his descendants leprosy.

As Elisha's servant, Gehazi was likely next in line to become a prophet, but he allowed his greed to get the best of him. Gehazi never stopped to ask why Elisha didn't accept the gifts. He didn't stop to think about any possible consequences for his actions. He just saw what he wanted and went for it. Instead of being able to enjoy the money and gifts that he essentially stole, Gehazi suffered the consequences of his actions for the rest of his life.

REFLECTION: Gehazi's story shows us that even those who serve God can be led astray by their unchecked desires. Greed, lust, and the pursuit of power can blind us to consequences and pull us away from God's will. We cannot serve both God and our desires.

Let this story be a warning. Either we will choose to follow God's will, or we'll face the consequences of following our desires.

TODAY'S PRAYER: Father, I ask that You guard my heart against greed. Help me to be content with what I have. Change my mindset so that I will be more focused on serving You than gaining earthly possessions. Amen.

The Floating Ax Head

Read II Kings 6:1-7

SUMMARY: Elisha was with a group of prophets cutting down trees. As one of the men was cutting a tree, his ax head fell into the river. He was very upset because he had borrowed the ax. Elisha cut a stick and threw it into the water where the ax had fallen. The ax head floated to the surface, and the man grabbed it.

Compared to most of the miracles in the Bible, this one probably seems insignificant. Sure, the man felt bad about losing the ax, but it wasn't a life-or-death situation. Yet, God sent a prophet to help with the minor issue.

REFLECTION: Sometimes we feel like we can't go to God with our problems because they seem insignificant compared to the big problems we see in the world. Be encouraged: God cares about the little things. The same God who created the universe is attentive to what worries you. The same God who is all-powerful delights in seeing you joyful.

Take time today to notice and appreciate the small blessings in your life—whether it's a beautiful day, a safe commute, or a kind word from someone. Remember, each of these moments is a gift from God.

TODAY'S PRAYER: Father, thank You for caring about every detail of my life, big and small. Teach me to bring everything to You in prayer, and fill my heart with gratitude for the little ways You show Your love each day. Amen.

Elisha Traps the Arameans

Read II Kings 6:8-23

SUMMARY: The king of Aram was at war with Israel. Every time he made battle plans, Elisha the prophet would warn the king of Israel, so they could be on alert. The king of Aram assumed that one of his officers was informing the king of Israel, but they told him that Elisha was to blame. One night, the king of Aram sent an army to surround the city where Elisha was. The next morning, Elisha and his servant saw them, and the servant was afraid. The Lord struck the army with blindness, and Elisha went outside and led the men to a different city.

Elisha noticed the anxiousness of his servant, and he prayed that the servant's eyes would be opened. Elisha wasn't speaking of the servant's physical eyes, but rather his spiritual eyes. Elisha wanted the servant to understand that there was no need to fear because they were on the Lord's side. While there were only two of them physically present, they were being protected by the Lord's army.

REFLECTION: When you face unexpected challenges and feel yourself becoming upset or anxious, try shifting your perspective. With your physical eyes, it may seem that defeat is inevitable, but remember that the Lord is fighting for you. You can be confident that the battle is fixed in your favor.

TODAY'S PRAYER: Father, when anxious thoughts attempt to cloud my mind, and I become overwhelmed by the cares of this world, I ask that You open my spiritual eyes so that I may see how You are working on my behalf. Amen.

Famine and Unbelief

Read II Kings 6:24-7:20

SUMMARY: After Israel's capital city was besieged by Aram, the price of food was inflated. Times were difficult for the people to the point that some became cannibals. The king blamed God and ordered that the prophet Elisha be killed. Elisha prophesied that the food supply would drastically increase the next day, but the king's officer did not believe him. As a result, Elisha told him that he would get to see the food, but he would not be able to eat it.

God delivered Israel through four lepers who discovered the abandoned Aramean camp filled with food and goods. They reported the news, and the people plundered the camp. Just as Elisha said, food prices dropped, and the doubting officer was trampled to death.

REFLECTION: Like the lepers, God often blesses us with more than we need. The question is, when we are blessed with abundance, do we share what we have with others, or do we hoard the blessings for ourselves? God desires that we share our abundance with others. This doesn't just apply to material things, but knowledge and other resources as well.

Think about the ways that God has blessed you recently. Is there something that you can share with someone in need? Choose to be a blessing to someone else and watch God continue to bless you.

TODAY'S PRAYER: Father, I thank You for the many blessings that You have given me. Show me ways that I can bless someone else. Amen

Hazael and King Ben-hadad

Read II Kings 8:7-15

SUMMARY: King Ben-hadad was very sick. He found out that Elisha was in the area, so he sent a high-ranking official named Hazael to ask Elisha if he would recover. Elisha told Hazael to tell King Ben-hadad that he would recover, although the Lord showed Elisha that he would still die. Elisha also told Hazael that he would become the next king of Aram, and wept after God showed him the harm Hazael would bring to Israel. The next day, Hazael suffocated King Ben-hadad and became the next king of Aram.

Hazael was stunned by Elisha's words and believed himself incapable of such evil. Yet, without seeking God, he took matters into his own hands and became a murderer.

REFLECTION: Like Hazael, we often believe our intentions are pure and that we are incapable of great harm. His story reminds us that without Christ, we act in the flesh and are capable of selfish and sinful choices. A lack of clear instruction is never permission to act apart from God. Let us commit to including God in every decision and draw closer to Him instead of relying on our own understanding.

TODAY'S PRAYER: Father, I realize that without You, I am liable to do things with selfish motives. Help me to include You in all of my decision-making. Amen.

Jehu is Anointed King of Israel

Read II Kings 9:1-29

SUMMARY: Elisha sent a prophet to anoint Jehu as king over Israel, declaring that God would use him to destroy the family of Ahab. After Jehu shared the message, his companions honored him by spreading their cloaks before him. Jehu immediately carried out God's judgment by killing King Joram of Israel and King Ahaziah of Judah, both connected to Ahab's family.

Being anointed as king was special. It was a sign that the person had been divinely appointed and prepared for the role. The anointing was never meant for personal edification, but for the purpose of accomplishing God's plan.

REFLECTION: Has God revealed what He has anointed you to do? The best way to walk in your purpose is to be in alignment with God's will. This alignment comes through prayer, studying Scripture, fellowship, and surrender. You may also find more clarity through fasting and fellowshipping with believers. When God has a plan for your life, He will make sure that you are clear on what He wants you to do. He may not reveal the entire plan all at once, but when you trust Him every step of the way, you cannot fail.

TODAY'S PRAYER: Father, I know that You have a plan for me and a purpose for my life. I ask that You help me to be in alignment with You so that I can be prepared for what You have anointed me to do. Amen.

The Death of Jezebel

Read II Kings 9:30-37

SUMMARY: Jehu arrived in Jezreel and instructed some eunuchs to throw Jezebel out of the window of her palace. When they threw her out of the window, Jehu's horses trampled her body under their feet. Later, Jehu instructed someone to bury her properly since Jezebel was the daughter of a king. When they went to bury her, they only found her feet, hands, and skull. Jezebel's body was eaten by dogs just as Elijah had prophesied. Though much time had passed since the prophecy, God's justice was ultimately fulfilled.

REFLECTION: Jezebel's end powerfully illustrates the truth that no one escapes the consequences of their actions. For years, she promoted wickedness, abused power, and led others into sin. Though judgment did not come immediately, what she sowed eventually produced a harvest. God's timing may have seemed slow, but His justice was never absent.

While this truth warns us against persistent sin, it also challenges us to examine our own lives. What seeds are we planting through our choices, words, and attitudes? Are we sowing bitterness or grace, pride or humility, rebellion or obedience? The harvest may not come today, but it will come.

TODAY'S PRAYER: Father, remind me that every choice I make is a seed that will one day bear fruit. Help me to sow seeds of righteousness, humility, and obedience, even when no one is watching, and the reward seems far away. Amen.

Jehu Kills Ahab's Family

Read II Kings 10:1-17

SUMMARY: The officials of Samaria were caring for King Ahab's seventy sons when Jehu sent a letter challenging them to defend Ahab's dynasty. Fearing Jehu, who had already killed two kings, they refused. Jehu then demanded the heads of Ahab's sons, and the officials complied. Jehu went on to eliminate the rest of Ahab's family and supporters in Jezreel and Samaria, fulfilling God's judgment.

Jehu obeyed God with boldness and urgency. When the prophet told Jehu to kill, Jehu killed. He didn't need a sign from God; the anointing was enough.

REFLECTION: How do we handle the responsibilities that God has given us? Do we respond swiftly, or do we allow things to linger as we wait for signs and confirmation? While it is completely normal to have some hesitation and to desire confirmation, at some point in our relationship with God, the anointing should be enough. As our faith matures, we learn to trust God and act boldly when He speaks. Let us continue to exercise our faith in small acts of obedience, and over time, our confidence in God will grow.

TODAY'S PRAYER: Father, I thank You that the responsibilities that You give me not only uplift Your kingdom, but they also develop my character. Help me to continue to trust You as You transform me into who You have called me to be. I pray that as my faith increases, my desire to execute Your plan will grow as well. Amen.

Jehu Kills the Priests of Baal

Read II Kings 10:18-36

SUMMARY: Jehu tricked the prophets and worshippers of Baal into coming together by pretending that he wanted to worship Baal. Jehu's officers then killed everyone in the temple and destroyed every trace of Baal worship in Israel. The Lord was pleased with Jehu's obedience in destroying the family of Ahab and promised to make his descendants kings of Israel.

Though Jehu was anointed and willing to serve, his obedience was selective. He fulfilled his calling but failed to live a righteous life, showing that being used by God is not the same as walking closely with Him.

REFLECTION: We must be careful as Christians not to confuse being used by God with having a relationship with God. Even the devil is used by God, so it's not an indicator of being close to Him. God desires our whole heart, not a partial commitment. We must examine our hearts daily to make sure that we are still submitting to Him. While it is amazing to live out your purpose here on earth, it's important to remember that your work here is only temporary. Your life in Jesus is eternal.

TODAY'S PRAYER: Father, I am humbled when You choose to use me, but I don't want that to be the extent of our relationship. I desire to go beyond the superficial and have a deeper connection with You. I want to understand You and live a life of righteousness. Amen.

Joash Repairs the Temple

Read II Kings 12:1-16

SUMMARY: Joash became the king of Judah when he was only seven years old. He was mentored by a priest named Jehoiada, and he was faithful to God while Jehoiada was alive. He noticed that the temple needed repair, so he had the priests and the Levites collect an offering to restore it. When progress stalled and the funds were misused, Joash placed a chest at the temple entrance so the people could give directly toward the repairs.

The state of the temple reflected the spiritual state of the people of Judah. They were worshiping and making sacrifices to idols. They had lost sight of God, and as a result, they had not invested in taking care of the temple.

REFLECTION: How does the place where you worship look? Is it clean and organized, or is it in need of updates and repairs? One of the ways that we can honor God is by taking care of our places of worship. The church shouldn't have to beg its members to tidy up after service or contribute to the building fund. The members should want their place of worship to be at its best because they want to honor God. Think about what you can do or how you can help to meet a need at your church.

TODAY'S PRAYER: Father, I am grateful for having a place where I can worship You and fellowship with other believers. Reveal to me any needs at my church that haven't been met and show me ways to make my church better. Amen.

Joash Turns From God

Read II Chronicles 24:17-27

SUMMARY: After the priest Jehoiada died, the leaders of Judah influenced King Joash to abandon the Lord and return to idol worship. The Lord sent prophets to warn Joash and the leaders about their sin, but they refused to listen. Finally, Zechariah, the son of Jehoiada, rebuked Joash and the leaders for their disobedience. They became angry and stoned Zechariah to death. Later, the Lord permitted the Arameans to invade Judah. Joash was wounded and eventually assassinated by his own officials as judgment for his actions.

Joash's quick shift from obedience to idolatry reveals that his faith was not personal. He followed God only while under Jehoiada's guidance, not from a genuine relationship of his own.

REFLECTION: It's safe to say that for most of us, our Christian journey started with compliance. Our parents or grandparents made us go to church. We were instructed to say our prayers. While that foundation can be helpful, it cannot sustain us forever. Our family and friends cannot get us into heaven. We must decide to have our own relationship with God. We must be intentional about seeking Him and knowing Him for ourselves.

TODAY'S PRAYER: Father, I long for a deeper relationship with You. I pray that Your Word would take root in my heart and guide my thoughts and actions. Amen.

Israel is Exiled

Read II Kings 17

SUMMARY: Israel was attacked by Assyria and forced to pay them money. After a while, the king of Israel rebelled and stopped sending money to Assyria. The king of Assyria captured and imprisoned the king of Israel, and he invaded Israel. The people of Israel were exiled to Assyria.

The king of Assyria then allowed foreigners to settle in Samaria (a city in Israel) to replace the people of Israel. The new residents did not worship the Lord, so the Lord sent lions among them, and some were killed. The king of Assyria then sent an exiled priest back to Samaria to teach the foreigners about God, but the foreigners continued to worship their idols in addition to worshiping God.

REFLECTION: Have you ever met people who mix religions—observing a few laws from one and adopting practices from another? While they may feel content doing whatever pleases them, God's Word is clear about where He stands. We cannot live with divided allegiance. God calls us to make a choice. If we choose to serve Him, we must serve Him alone. Anything less is ultimately a rejection of His authority.

TODAY'S PRAYER: Father, forgive me for the times that I have attempted to alter or ignore certain parts of Your Word because it didn't align with how I wanted to live my life. I realize that Your Word will not change, and anything You command is for my good. I choose to serve You completely and honor that. Amen.

Hezekiah Seeks the Lord

Read II Kings 18:1-19:37

SUMMARY: King Hezekiah received a message from the king of Assyria threatening to invade Jerusalem. Distressed, Hezekiah first sent men to the prophet Isaiah for guidance, and Isaiah assured him that Jerusalem would not be harmed. When a second threatening letter arrived, Hezekiah went directly to the Lord in prayer, asking Him to deliver the city so that all nations would know His power. That night, the angel of the Lord struck down 185,000 Assyrian soldiers, and the king of Assyria withdrew.

The contrast between the two responses is significant. After the first message, Hezekiah relied on Isaiah and referred to the Lord as "thy God." After the second, he personally sought the Lord, exalted Him, acknowledged His power, and asked for His help in faith.

REFLECTION: Hezekiah was aware of God's power through Isaiah, but this experience caused him to know God for himself. His experience helped him to understand that he didn't need a prophet to reach God. The Lord listened to him as well. Similarly, we sometimes have to experience trials and tribulations so that we can draw closer to the Lord. This reminds us that God desires a personal faith—one that comes to Him directly in times of fear and need.

TODAY'S PRAYER: Father, help me to come directly to You when I am afraid. Strengthen my faith so that I may trust You fully and acknowledge You as my God. I place my fears before You and ask that You be glorified through my life. Amen.

Hezekiah's Sickness and Recovery

Read II Kings 20:1-11

SUMMARY: Hezekiah became very ill and received word from the prophet Isaiah that he would die. Hezekiah prayed to the Lord and then broke down and cried. Before Isaiah left the palace, the Lord told him to go back to Hezekiah and let him know that He heard his prayer and would add fifteen years to his life. Isaiah then instructed Hezekiah's servants to apply an ointment made from figs to the boil, and Hezekiah recovered.

REFLECTION: This story offers many lessons, but one stands out: God can work through medicine. The ointment did not replace God's healing power—it was the means He chose to use. This reminds us that trusting in God's healing and accepting medical treatment are not opposing beliefs. Medicine may be the very method God uses to bring healing. When doctors recommend treatment, it is wise to prayerfully consider it, seek understanding, and trust that God can use any vessel to accomplish His plans.

TODAY'S PRAYER: Father, thank You for Your healing power. I ask that You keep my family healthy. Guide our doctors as they make decisions for our good. I pray that any treatments that I receive will be vessels for restoration. Amen.

The Discovery of God's Law

Read II Kings 22

SUMMARY: During King Josiah's 18th year as king, he decided to repair the temple. During the renovation process, Hilkiah, the high priest, found the Book of the Law of the Lord. The book was brought to the king, and when he read it, he tore his clothing in distress. He realized that his ancestors had not been obeying the laws. He sent men to inquire of the Lord, and they consulted Huldah the prophetess. She warned the men that God would curse the land due to the disobedience of the people, but because Josiah repented, the judgment would not happen until after he died.

REFLECTION: For us to live a life of righteousness, we have to read the book that contains God's laws. We must be aware of God's commandments. We must be aware of how Christ lived so that we can follow His example. We must be aware of the mistakes made by others so that we do not repeat them.

Reflect on today: have you ever suffered consequences due to not reading God's Word? How can you do a better job of studying the Bible?

TODAY'S PRAYER: Father, thank You for giving us Your Word, the Bible. As I study it, I ask that You open my ears and heart to hear what You are saying to me. Grant me understanding and guide me in Your truth. Amen.

Judah is Exiled

Read II Kings 24

SUMMARY: King Jehoiakim of Judah rebelled against Babylon, and the Lord allowed raiders from several nations, including Babylon, to destroy Judah. When Jehoiakim's son Jehoiachin became king, the officers of Babylon took control of the capital city, Jerusalem. They exiled Jehoiachin along with several officials and elite workers of Judah to Babylon. The king of Babylon allowed the poorest people to remain in Judah, and he made Jehoiachin's uncle, Zedekiah, the new king of Judah.

In II Kings 17, the Lord allowed the northern kingdom of Israel to be exiled, and now in II Kings 24, the Lord allowed the same thing to happen in Judah. The Lord had been sending people to warn the Israelites about being disobedient since the book of Deuteronomy. The warnings can also be found in the books of Amos, Ezekiel, Jeremiah, Micah, and Nehemiah.

REFLECTION: We are so blessed to serve a God who is quick to forgive and slow to punish. He gives us chance after chance to get things right, but far too often we take his goodness and his mercy for granted. If we continue to sin, however, we may have to suffer the consequences of our actions. Let us be mindful to take heed to God's warnings before it's too late. May we get to a point where we pursue a life of righteousness, not out of fear of consequences, but because of how much we love our God.

TODAY'S PRAYER: Father, I thank You for being patient with me and my sin. Help me to be sensitive to Your warnings and continue to walk in Your ways. Amen.

The Temple is Destroyed

Read II Kings 25:1-26

SUMMARY: Zedekiah, the appointed king of Judah, eventually rebelled against King Nebuchadnezzar, so the king led his army against Jerusalem. They built siege ramps to block any business or trade, and eventually, the people in the city experienced a famine. The Babylonian army burned down the temple and all of the houses in Jerusalem. They tore down the walls of Jerusalem and took more people back to Babylon as exiles. Nebuchadnezzar appointed Gedaliah as governor over those left in Judah. Gedaliah encouraged the people to live peacefully and rebuild, but he ignored warnings about a threat from a man named Ishmael and was killed as a result.

REFLECTION: While it is great to see the best in everyone, the Bible is very clear about being vigilant and on guard against the enemy (I Peter 5:8). Everyone has some good in them, but that doesn't mean that their intentions towards you are good. Not everyone will be happy when you elevate in life. Not everyone will support you in your calling. Gedaliah's story reminds us to listen to wise counsel and guard our hearts. We can live with integrity without placing ourselves in unnecessary danger.

TODAY'S PRAYER: Father, I pray that You allow me to balance seeing the good in people while guarding myself against bad intentions. Give me discernment to know who I can trust. Give me wisdom to know when to be cautious. Amen.

The Prayer of Jabez

Read I Chronicles 4:9-10

SUMMARY: In I Chronicles, we read about an honorable man named Jabez who prayed a short but powerful prayer that God answered. His prayer included four requests: for God's blessing, acknowledging Him as the source of all he needed; for expanded territory, reflecting a desire for growth; for God's hand to be with him, seeking guidance and alignment with God's will; and for protection from evil, recognizing his need for God's continued care.

REFLECTION: Sometimes we can feel like our prayers aren't good enough. We feel as if God won't answer our prayers because our words are too simple or the prayer isn't long enough. Jabez's prayer shows us that God hears and answers even the simplest prayers. When you communicate with God, don't worry so much about the eloquence of what you are saying. Focus on the sincerity behind your prayer. Be honest with God about what you desire. Approach Him with humility, understanding that He is an all-powerful God. Trust that He is listening and will give you the desires of your heart.

TODAY'S PRAYER: Father, I thank You for always listening when I pray. I ask that You bless me so that I can be a blessing to others. I pray for even greater opportunities to serve You, and I pray that Your presence will never leave me. Protect me from dangers seen and unseen. Amen.

War with Surrounding Nations

Read II Chronicles 20

SUMMARY: The armies of Ammon, Moab, and Mount Seir joined together to attack Judah. When King Jehoshaphat heard the news, he was scared. He called the people together to fast and pray. A man named Jahaziel prophesied that the victory was theirs. They would not even need to fight. King Jehoshaphat and the people of Judah and Jerusalem all worshiped the Lord. The next morning, Jehoshaphat and his army went out to battle, singing and giving praise. As they were singing, the enemies started fighting amongst themselves. As a result, the surrounding nations feared the Lord, and Judah experienced peace.

Jehoshaphat gives us a great example of how to respond to anxiety. When he felt worried, he immediately went to God for direction and led his people not only to pray, but to fast. Jehoshaphat humbled himself and acknowledged that he couldn't defeat the armies out of his own strength but only with the help of God. Despite the worry, he worshiped.

REFLECTION: Sometimes, when dealing with anxiety, it can be hard to focus on anything but the situation you're in, but try turning to God. He is with you, and He will show you what to do. Remember the times when He helped you in the past. Surrender your problem to Him and praise Him in advance for the victory!

TODAY'S PRAYER: Father, I thank You that the battles I face are not mine to fight. I will turn my troubles over to You and claim the victory. Amen.

King Amaziah

Read II Chronicles 25

SUMMARY: When Amaziah became king of Judah, he did what was right in the Lord's sight but was not fully devoted to Him. He raised an army that included soldiers from Israel, but after a prophet warned that the Lord was not with Israel, Amaziah sent them away. God granted Amaziah victory over the Edomites, yet afterward he brought home their idols and began to worship them. His pride later led him to challenge Jehoash, king of Israel, resulting in defeat and his capture.

After the Lord showed Himself mighty to Amaziah and allowed him to defeat the Edomites, Amaziah chose to serve the Edomites' idol gods. Even when confronted by a prophet, his actions revealed a divided heart and misplaced trust.

REFLECTION: Like Amaziah, we can be tempted to turn to modern "idols" that promise comfort but offer no true victory. Whether it is substances, relationships, or other distractions, these idols cannot save or satisfy. Only God is faithful and powerful enough to give lasting victory and restoration.

TODAY'S PRAYER: Father, thank You for Your faithfulness in my life. Forgive me for the times I have placed temporary things above You, and help me to trust You alone. Amen.

Uzziah Rules in Judah

Read II Chronicles 26

SUMMARY: Uzziah became king when he was sixteen years old. He started his reign by doing right and seeking guidance from the Lord. As a result, he became very famous and powerful. Eventually, he grew proud and overstepped his God-given authority by performing duties reserved for the priests. When confronted, he became angry, and the Lord struck him with leprosy. Uzziah lived in isolation until his death.

Uzziah's downfall was rooted in pride. Though he held great power, he ignored the boundaries God had set and rejected correction from those in authority. As a result, he quickly faced the consequences of his actions.

REFLECTION: King Uzziah's story reminds us of the importance of humility. You may hold a position of authority or influence—at work, in an organization, or within the church—but no matter your role, we are all accountable to God and to one another. No single person is meant to be in charge of everything. In fact, healthy systems of checks and balances are a gift, helping ensure accountability and integrity. Make it a priority to respect the roles of others and the boundaries God has put in place.

TODAY'S PRAYER: Father, thank You for reminding me that all authority comes from You. Guard my heart against pride, and help me walk in humility no matter the position You place me in. Teach me to respect the roles and boundaries You have established and to welcome accountability with a willing spirit. Amen.

The Temple is Rebuilt

Read Ezra 3

SUMMARY: After returning from exile, the Israelites rebuilt the altar and began reconstructing the temple. When the foundation was laid, the younger people rejoiced, while older leaders wept because they remembered the former temple's grandeur.

A lot of effort was put into the original temple. David had given Solomon the building plans and had provided resources to create a lavish space. The only problem was that the size and grandeur of the building didn't make the people holier. The people of Israel continued to sin and do as they pleased until they were exiled. When they returned to Jerusalem, however, they came with a desire to live righteously. The new building may not have been as nice as before, but the people now had hearts for God.

REFLECTION: Sometimes, we focus on outward appearances while neglecting our spiritual condition. We quote a few scriptures and claim to be a Christian, but we can't remember the last time that we went to church or had a conversation with God. We put God in second place while we continue to do things that satisfy our flesh. What matters most to God is not how impressive we appear, but the posture of our hearts. He desires obedience, righteousness, and a genuine relationship with us.

TODAY'S PRAYER: Father, I pray that I would be more concerned with my heart posture than I am with my outward appearance. Amen.

Nehemiah Goes to Jerusalem

Read Nehemiah 2

SUMMARY: Nehemiah, a cupbearer to the king of Persia, was saddened by the condition of Jerusalem. After praying, he asked the king for permission to return and rebuild the city. The king agreed to his request and provided him with letters for safe passage and resources. Nehemiah did not reveal the plans that God had given him to anyone until he took some time to inspect the walls surrounding the city. After inspecting, he then brought the plan to some of the Jewish leaders, and they were agreeable. Nehemiah was clear on the assignment that God had given him, but he also understood the importance of proper planning before implementation.

REFLECTION: Nehemiah shows us that God-given assignments require both prayer and planning. Excitement alone isn't enough—we must take time to assess the situation, seek God's guidance, and be wise about who we share our plans with. Not everyone will understand or support what God is calling you to do. Pray, plan carefully, and move forward with excellence and discernment.

TODAY'S PRAYER: Father, help me to be patient and intentional with the plans You've given me. Give me wisdom, clarity, and discernment as I move forward. Amen.

Opposition to the Walls: Part I

Read Nehemiah 4

SUMMARY: Nehemiah and the Jews were halfway done with the wall, and this angered their enemies. The enemies began to mock them and made plans to attack them. The Jews prayed, stayed alert, and continued working. They kept swords at their sides, with half the men working and half ready to fight, knowing the threat could return at any time.

REFLECTION: Nehemiah and his men provide an excellent example for Christians today. When God gives us an assignment for the kingdom, we should always expect opposition and attacks from the enemy. Like the men, we have to be able to balance completing our assigned tasks and staying on guard. We may not be aware of when the attacks will come or how they will come, so we should always be prepared. The Bible is our sword. We must study it so that we will be able to cut through any lies, temptation, or deception that would hinder us from executing God's plan. We can't allow the spiritual attacks to distract or discourage us from doing what God has called us to do. We must remain encouraged and keep our minds on the Lord.

TODAY'S PRAYER: Father, help me to remain alert and strong in the face of opposition. Thank You for protecting me and guiding me as I do Your work. Amen.

Nehemiah Defends the Oppressed

Read Nehemiah 5

SUMMARY: Many of the Israelites were experiencing hard times due to a famine. This was only made worse by financial hardships put on them by nobles who charged interest on loans and essentially forced children into slavery. Nehemiah found out about the oppression of the people and confronted the nobles. He called a meeting and demanded that the nobles stop charging interest and return what they had taken. The nobles agreed to comply with Nehemiah's demands.

REFLECTION: So often, people accept leadership positions with the mindset of what a new level or status can do for them, but Nehemiah shows us how that shouldn't be the case. Leadership is about understanding the burdens of the less fortunate. Leadership is about defending people from those who would try to use them. Leadership is about sacrificing your desires for the greater good. May we all be mindful to consider our intentions and the cost of leadership before we make the decision to lead.

TODAY'S PRAYER: Father, help me to lead with humility and selflessness, placing the needs of others above my own. Amen.

Opposition to the Walls: Part II

Read Nehemiah 6

SUMMARY: Sanballat, Tobiah, and Geshem heard that the wall of Jerusalem was nearly finished, so they sent messengers to Nehemiah four times asking him to meet. Nehemiah understood their intent to harm him and declined. The fifth time, Sanballat sent an open letter threatening to accuse the Jews of rebellion to the king of Persia. They even sent a prophet to warn Nehemiah to hide. Despite these threats, Nehemiah pressed on, and the Jews completed the wall in fifty-two days.

REFLECTION: Sometimes, when we face obstacles, it can be hard to tell whether it's God redirecting us or the devil blocking us. That's where our discernment should kick in. Take time to evaluate things, and don't be afraid to ask God for confirmation. If you believe that God is directing you to complete the task at hand, then continue to push through. Opposition may come to intimidate and distract you, but use the enemies' roadblocks to push you to work harder. The enemy may even send trusted individuals to discourage you, but remember that not everyone is privy to your conversations with God. Know that if God has blessed you to do a task, He will give you the grace to complete it (Ephesians 2:10). Just keep pressing to the finish line.

TODAY'S PRAYER: Father, thank You for trusting me with the work You've given me. Grant me discernment to navigate challenges and the strength to complete my assignments. Amen.

Nehemiah's Reforms

Read Nehemiah 13

SUMMARY: Nehemiah returned to Persia after his time in Jerusalem ended, but later came back to see how the people were doing. He discovered that they had returned to sinful habits. An enemy was living in the temple, tithing had stopped, the Sabbath was being ignored, and Jewish men were marrying foreign women. Nehemiah was shocked and angered by their disregard for God's covenant. He confronted the leaders and put rules in place to restore order and lead the people back to God.

After being removed from exile for some time, the people had grown comfortable and slowly drifted away from obedience. Thankfully, God remained faithful and sent Nehemiah back to correct them. Nehemiah's approach was firm and direct, but it was necessary.

REFLECTION: How do you respond when someone confronts your sin? Do you humble yourself and repent, or do you become defensive? While gentle correction is often appropriate, there are times when firm confrontation is needed. It can be hard to receive, but consider the source. Does this person care about you? Are they sensitive to God's leading? If so, choose humility. Receive the correction, turn away from sin, and thank God for the opportunity to realign with Him.

TODAY'S PRAYER: Father, give me discernment to recognize the "Nehemiahs" in my life who only desire to see me live for You. Help me to remain humble and open to correction. Amen.

Job's First Test

Read Job 1

SUMMARY: Job was known as a blameless and upright man. He had a large family and great wealth. One day, Satan claimed that Job only served God because of his blessings. God allowed Satan to test Job by taking away his possessions, but not harming him physically. In a single day, Job lost his livestock, servants, and all of his children. Despite his immense loss, Job did not blame God. Instead, he worshiped Him.

REFLECTION: Could you respond like Job if everything you had was taken away? Job declared, "The Lord gave, and the Lord hath taken away; blessed be the name of the Lord." He understood that everything he had came from God. Though deeply grieved, he remained grateful for what God had given him.

Our faith will be tested, regardless of how righteous we try to live. While it is normal to feel pain and sorrow, we must still choose gratitude. Praise God for life, remember His past faithfulness, and thank Him in advance for restoration. As Scripture reminds us, in everything give thanks (1 Thessalonians 5:18).

TODAY'S PRAYER: Father, help me to maintain a heart of gratitude. Even in difficult moments, remind me of all the reasons I have to be thankful. Amen.

Job's Second Test

Read Job 2:1-10

SUMMARY: Once again, Satan presented himself before the Lord, and Job's name was mentioned. This time, Satan claimed that Job was only devoted to God because, despite losing his possessions, he still had his health. God then allowed Satan to take away Job's health, but he had to spare Job's life. Satan left the presence of the Lord and caused Job to have boils all over this body. His wife encouraged him to "curse God, and die," but Job never said anything against God.

Notice that God submitted Job's name to Satan, but Satan couldn't take away Job's possessions until God permitted him. Even in that, Satan still could not touch Job. Then, God allowed Satan to curse Job with an illness, but Satan still could not kill Job. Every challenge was under God's control.

REFLECTION: In life, we will endure tough times and tough tests, but we must remember that no matter how hard life gets, God is in control. There is no need to fear the devil because he can only do what God allows. Any test that we experience has been approved by God, and He will never give us a challenge that we can't handle through Him. So when the tests of life start to overwhelm you, find hope in the fact that you know the Teacher. Draw close to God and trust that what you're going through is only temporary. Better days are ahead.

TODAY'S PRAYER: Father, I acknowledge that I cannot overcome the tests of life alone. I need Your guidance and strength. Help me to persevere through every obstacle and to find comfort in Your presence. Amen.

Job's Friends Support Him

Read Job 2:11-13

SUMMARY: Three of Job's friends heard about his suffering and came to comfort him. When they arrived, they hardly recognized Job and were deeply grieved. Instead of speaking, they sat with him in silence for seven days and seven nights.

Although Job's friends could not fully relate to his loss, they showed up to support him. They paused their lives and chose presence over words. They could not change his circumstances, but they remained by his side during his pain.

REFLECTION: When those we love are hurting, it can be difficult to know what to say. We may feel pressured to offer advice, encouragement, or Scripture. Yet Job's story reminds us that sometimes the greatest ministry is simply being present. People may not remember what you said in their darkest moment, but they will remember that you were there. They will recall how you showed up for them and how that made them feel.

Our loved ones are God's gift to us. In their time of need, we should remind them that they are not alone. Don't worry about being awkward. Don't worry about saying the wrong thing. Just be present.

TODAY'S PRAYER: Father, I pray that You allow me to be a source of comfort to my friends and family when they are down. Fill me with Your love and peace so that I can share that with them in their time of need. Amen.

The Lord Blesses Job

Read Job 42:7-17

SUMMARY: The Lord was angry with Job's friends for misrepresenting Him, so He instructed them to have Job pray on their behalf. Job prayed for them, and the Lord restored everything that he had lost, giving him twice as much as he had before. Job was able to give an inheritance to all of his children, and he lived a long life.

Although Job's story ends with restoration, it does not erase the pain he endured. His children who died would never return, and the memories of his suffering remained. In verse 11, Scripture tells us that Job's family and friends came to comfort him and brought gifts because of all he had endured. Job did not have to pretend that everything was fine. He was allowed to mourn his losses while still embracing the goodness of his present season.

REFLECTION: We often assume that once we reach the other side of hardship, everything will instantly feel better. But healing can take time. You may experience joy and gratitude while still carrying pain from the past. God wants you to know that you don't have to act like everything is okay. It's okay to take time to heal, to lean on others, and to process what you've been through. You can celebrate your victories while still recovering from the battles that brought you there.

TODAY'S PRAYER: Father, give me the strength and wisdom to heal the parts of me that are still hurting. Help me to process my past and guide me to the people You have placed in my life for support. Amen.

Queen Vashti

Read Esther 1

SUMMARY: King Xerxes held an extravagant banquet to display his wealth and power. During the feast, he ordered Queen Vashti to appear before his guests so they could admire her beauty. Vashti refused the king's command, which angered him and embarrassed him in front of his officials. After consulting his advisers, the king removed Vashti from her position as queen and banished her from the kingdom.

Scripture notes that the king was in high spirits from wine when he made the request, suggesting that his judgment was impaired. In that moment, he treated Vashti as an object rather than honoring her as queen.

REFLECTION: People's circumstances and emotions can affect how they treat us. In moments of anger, fear, or poor judgment, they may overlook our dignity or disregard our boundaries. That is why it is sometimes necessary to say "no," even when it is difficult. Setting boundaries can come with consequences, but it also protects your integrity and can empower others to do the same. As believers, our choices can influence those watching. Be willing to stand firm and honor God by honoring yourself.

TODAY'S PRAYER: Father, give me wisdom and courage to set healthy boundaries. Help me to communicate them with clarity and grace. Amen.

Esther Becomes Queen

Read Esther 2

SUMMARY: After Queen Vashti was banished, King Xerxes' attendants suggested that he find a new wife. Many virgins were brought to the king's harem, including Mordecai's cousin Esther. Mordecai and Esther were Jewish, but Mordecai advised Esther to keep this a secret. After an extensive process, Esther was chosen to be the queen.

The Bible says that Esther had the favor of everyone she met. At every turn, she was admired and given special privileges. Opportunities seemed to come easily for her, but what had she done that was so special? The answer is nothing. Esther had been chosen by God for this moment. She didn't have to do anything to stand out because He was working on her behalf. There was no need to stress or worry about how to become the queen because it was already done.

REFLECTION: If God has called you to do something, your job is to remain obedient and trust in Him. You don't have to stress yourself out or worry about whether you are good enough. He will provide you with unmerited favor. He causes doors to open, distinguishes you among others, and places the right people—like Mordecai and Hegai—along your path to help guide you. Rest in His promises. When God is for you, you already have everything you need.

TODAY'S PRAYER: Father, I thank You for Your unmerited favor. Help me not to worry about what I lack, but rather to trust that You will provide all my needs. I am confident that if I step out on faith and do what You have asked of me, You will allow me to prosper. Amen.

Haman's Plot Against the Jews

Read Esther 3

SUMMARY: Haman received a promotion from King Xerxes that included a mandate that the king's officials should bow down to him. Mordecai refused to bow down before Haman. Haman was upset with Mordecai's lack of respect and attempted to kill all of the Jews.

Haman was the second most powerful man in the kingdom, but even with all of that authority, he was insecure. Haman was a man who required constant validation. He needed to be noticed by others, and he desired their praise. So when Mordecai refused to bow down to him, he couldn't look past it. It was a huge blow to his ego. It wasn't enough to just take out his frustration on Mordecai; he decided to destroy Mordecai's entire community.

REFLECTION: Like Haman, we can be guilty of letting criticism or disapproval from one person overshadow all the support we receive. While we can't control others' opinions, we can choose where to place our focus. Reflect on encouragement, rather than negativity, and empower those who uplift you instead of giving power to the naysayers.

TODAY'S PRAYER: Father, thank You for the people who encourage and support me. Help me to ignore negativity and focus on the love and guidance You provide through those who care for me. Amen.

Mordecai Requests Esther's Help

Read Esther 4

SUMMARY: When the Jewish people heard about the decree to destroy all the Jews, they were distraught. Mordecai sent a message asking Esther to beg the king for mercy on behalf of her people. Esther was worried, as appearing before the king at the wrong time could cost her her life. She told Mordecai to gather all the Jews of the area to fast on her behalf.

REFLECTION: When we fast, we don't come to God with our Christmas list. This isn't our chance to ask for things that we want. The purpose of fasting is to turn away from the things that would normally distract us and focus our attention on God. We draw closer to Him and can better hear from Him. The Holy Spirit can convict us and direct us.

Is there something in your life that has been troubling you? Are you looking for clarity or confirmation? I encourage you to try fasting. Turn down your plate or take a break from social media. Put aside whatever takes up valuable time throughout the day and spend that time drawing closer to the Lord. Read Scripture, pray, worship, and then take time to be silent and hear what God has to say.

TODAY'S PRAYER: Father, I thank You that You know me and love me. I desire to know You as well. Forgive me for craving food or other things more than You. I pray that You would help me to turn to You and seek You above all else. Amen.

Haman Plans to Kill Mordecai

Read Esther 5

SUMMARY: On the third day of fasting, Esther approached the king, and he welcomed her in. She requested to have a banquet with him and Haman. At the banquet with the king and Haman, the king asked what she wanted, and Esther requested to have another banquet with them to finally reveal her request. Haman was very happy. He went home to brag to his wife and friends about attending the banquet. He also further expressed his disdain for Mordecai. His friends suggested that he set up a sharpened pole and ask the king to impale Mordecai on it. Haman did as they suggested.

There could have been several reasons why Esther was taking so long to state her request, and one possibility is that Esther was still afraid. Esther knew what she had been called to do; she had fasted and prayed, but there was still a small fear that her plan could go wrong.

REFLECTION: Have you ever felt this way? Maybe God called you to witness to a stranger, or He wanted you to sow a significant seed into your church. You know what you're supposed to do, but there's still that small drop of doubt that makes you hesitate to act.

Obedience doesn't always mean acting without fear—it means moving forward despite it. God understands your hesitation and honors your willingness to follow through, even when courage takes time.

TODAY'S PRAYER: Father, help me to obey You even when fear tries to delay my actions. Give me clarity, courage, and faith to trust You fully. Amen.

The King Honors Mordecai

Read Esther 6

SUMMARY: King Xerxes couldn't sleep, so he had the records of his reign read to him and discovered that Mordecai had once saved his life. Wanting to honor him, the king asked Haman for advice. Assuming the honor was for himself, Haman suggested a public display of royal praise—only to be ordered to carry it out for Mordecai instead. Haman left humiliated, realizing his plans were failing. Everything from the timing to the people involved worked for the good of Mordecai, and he wasn't even aware of it.

REFLECTION: Have you ever experienced the hand of God working things together in your life? God often works behind the scenes in ways we don't immediately recognize. What seems like a coincidence is often divine timing. Looking back, we can see how God arranged people, moments, and circumstances for our good. Even when we are unaware, God is faithfully working on our behalf. Trust the process and stay close to Him.

TODAY'S PRAYER: Father, help me to recognize Your hand at work in my life. Teach me to trust that You are always arranging things according to Your perfect will. Amen.

The King Executes Haman

Read Esther 7

SUMMARY: The king and Haman attended Esther's second banquet. Esther revealed Haman's plan to destroy the Jews and pleaded for their lives. Haman begged Esther for mercy and, in the process, fell on the couch where she was lying. The king's attendants took him away, and he was impaled on the pole that he had set up for Mordecai.

Haman's story shows us the importance of forgiveness. Mordecai disrespected him in Esther 3, and Haman was unable to let that go. There's a well-known quote that states, "forgiveness isn't for the other person, it's for you." Mordecai never asked for forgiveness, but Haman should have freely given it—not for Mordecai's benefit, but for his own.

REFLECTION: As Christians, we will experience times where people hurt us, sometimes for no apparent reason. We have to learn to forgive them. Harboring that hurt doesn't affect them; it affects us. Don't allow the pains of the past to ruin your present. Give it to the Lord. Ask Him to give you the strength to forgive and move on.

TODAY'S PRAYER: Father, I thank You for the gift of forgiveness. I ask that You help me to forgive others freely, just as you have forgiven me. Help me to let go of the grudges that I have held from past hurt. Allow me to move on in freedom. Amen.

Esther Helps the Jews

Read Esther 8

SUMMARY: After his death, Esther received Haman's property, and Mordecai received the king's ring. Once again, Esther asked King Xerxes to issue a decree to reverse Haman's order. King Xerxes allowed Esther and Mordecai to issue an order authorizing the Jews to defend themselves against anyone who tried to attack them. The Jews rejoiced and celebrated their victory.

Even after Haman's death, the decree that he had issued still loomed over the Jews' heads. At this point, both Esther and Mordecai were safe, but Esther still pleaded to the king on behalf of her people. Haman's decree couldn't be reversed, but Mordecai's new order made it so that no one would want to bother the Jews because they could end up getting hurt themselves. The Jews had freedom in spite of the old law.

REFLECTION: Just like Mordecai's decree saved the Jews, Jesus saved us. The old law said that we should die because of our sins, but Jesus took our place when He died on the cross. His sacrifice ensured that we wouldn't have to be bound by the old law. Just like the Jews, we can celebrate because we are free. Let us give thanks to God for His love and His grace.

TODAY'S PRAYER: Father, thank You for giving sinners like me a way to return to You. Without Your mercy, I would have been given the punishment that I deserve. Because You have given me a new life in You, I want to use it for Your glory. Amen.

Jeremiah's Call

Read Jeremiah 1

SUMMARY: Jeremiah was called by God to be a prophet to the Nations, but he felt that he could not speak for God because he was too young.

God never denied that Jeremiah was young, but instead He moved Jeremiah's focus from his shortcomings to God's power. God assured Jeremiah that He knew him and had a plan for him before he was born. God told Jeremiah not to be afraid and promised to be with him and protect him. God gave Jeremiah visions to prove that He was not only watching over him but that what He said would come to pass. Then, finally, God gave Jeremiah instructions so that he could carry out His plan. God acknowledged that there would be some pushback, but it would fail because God would take care of him.

REFLECTION: Like Jeremiah, we may feel unqualified or inexperienced, but God doesn't call us based on our ability—He equips us with His power. When doubt arises, shift your focus from what you lack to what God can do through you. Trust that He has prepared you for this moment.

TODAY'S PRAYER: Father, thank You for choosing me and trusting me with Your work. Remove my self-doubt and help me to walk confidently in what You have called me to do. Amen.

Hananiah Contradicts Jeremiah

Read Jeremiah 28

SUMMARY: A man named Hananiah falsely prophesied that within two years the Lord would return the people and vessels that had been taken to Babylon. He then broke the physical yoke that God had instructed Jeremiah to wear as a demonstration of God breaking the yoke of oppression. The Lord instructed the prophet Jeremiah to confront Hananiah, declaring that it was God Himself who had placed the nations under King Nebuchadnezzar's rule. Jeremiah prophesied that Hananiah would die within that year because he misled the people.

Jeremiah had been delivering warnings of judgment and exile for the people of Judah. In this story, Hananiah openly contradicted Jeremiah in front of everyone in the temple by giving the people a message of false hope. Even though Hananiah was aggressive and wrong, Jeremiah responded in humility and left. He knew that time would reveal who was telling the truth.

REFLECTION: Being falsely accused or corrected in public can stir anger and a desire to defend ourselves. Jeremiah shows us another way—patience, integrity, and trust in God. Sometimes walking away honors God more than winning an argument. The truth doesn't need our defense; God will reveal it in His time.

TODAY'S PRAYER: Father, help me to respond with grace when I am treated unfairly. Give me peace in trusting You to reveal the truth and protect my integrity. Amen.

Jeremiah Documents His Prophecies

Read Jeremiah 36

SUMMARY: The Lord instructed Jeremiah to start writing down all of the prophecies against Judah and the other nations. Jeremiah had a man named Baruch read the messages in the temple to the people. King Jehoiakim burned the scroll, but God instructed Jeremiah to rewrite it and add a warning of judgment for the king's actions.

The people of Judah had already heard Jeremiah's prophecies before, but God had Jeremiah write down the prophecies, just in case the people of Judah were ready to repent. The prophecies weren't given to scare the people, but rather to save them. God wanted them to know what was coming so that they could turn their lives around before it was too late.

REFLECTION: When God speaks, do you take time to preserve what He says? We can hear from God in so many ways, including sermons, Scripture, worship songs, or even prophecies. So often when we hear messages from God, we can get caught up and excited in the moment, only to forget what was said later on. Sometimes the messages that we receive are not relevant to our present, but vital for the future, so it's important that we keep the message somewhere where we can refer to it later. God isn't giving us a message for nothing. There is always a purpose behind His words.

TODAY'S PRAYER: Father, help me to value and remember Your words. Teach me to listen carefully and keep what You reveal so I can walk in obedience. Amen.

The Valley of Dry Bones

Read Ezekiel 37:1-14

SUMMARY: God gave Ezekiel a vision of a valley filled with dry bones and instructed him to prophesy over them. As Ezekiel obeyed, the bones came together, were covered with flesh, and were brought to life by the breath of God. The vision represented Israel, a people who felt cut off and hopeless in exile. God used this vision to show that He would restore them, bring them home, and remind them that He is the Lord.

Though Israel's situation seemed beyond repair because of their repeated disobedience, God demonstrated that even the most lifeless circumstances can be revived by His power.

REFLECTION: Have you ever experienced a "dry bones" season in your life? Have you ever experienced a point where you lost all hope in a situation? Whether it's a dream, a relationship, or your health, God can bring life where there appears to be none. Instead of giving up, speak life over your situation and trust in God's restoring power. What looks dead to you may be the very place where God reveals His glory.

TODAY'S PRAYER: Father, when I feel discouraged and hopeless, help me to trust in You. Breathe new life into the areas of my life that feel dry and restore my faith in Your power. Amen.

Daniel in Nebuchadnezzar's Court

Read Daniel 1

SUMMARY: The Lord allowed Babylon to conquer Jerusalem, and King Nebuchadnezzar took several young men—including Daniel and his three friends—to serve in the royal palace. Their names were changed, and they were trained in Babylonian culture. They were offered food and wine from the king's table, but Daniel and his friends chose to eat only vegetables and drink water, refusing food that violated God's law. God honored their faithfulness, and they became healthier, stronger, and wiser than the others, earning the king's favor.

Daniel may have been young, but he had a good sense of boundaries. He accepted cultural training and the name change, but he drew the line at eating unclean food. Daniel understood that if Scripture set the boundary, then he should do the same.

REFLECTION: How good are you at setting boundaries? Are you a strict "no means no" kind of person, or do you sometimes blur the lines and compromise? Setting boundaries is essential to living out our faith. When the values of the world conflict with God's Word, we must choose obedience. Standing firm does not require disrespect or judgment of others —it requires conviction. Like Daniel, we are called to honor God by remaining faithful, even when compromise feels easier.

TODAY'S PRAYER: Father, give me strength, wisdom, and courage to set and honor godly boundaries, while also respecting the boundaries of others. Amen.

Nebuchadnezzar's Dream

Read Daniel 2

SUMMARY: King Nebuchadnezzar had a troubling dream but refused to tell it to his wise men, demanding that they reveal both the dream and its meaning. When no one could, he ordered the execution of all the wise men, including Daniel and his friends. Daniel asked the king for time and urged his friends to pray with him. That night, God revealed the dream to Daniel in a vision. Daniel was able to tell the king the dream and reveal its meaning. As a result, Daniel's life was spared, he was promoted, and his friends were elevated as well.

This story shows the power of shared prayer. Instead of Daniel carrying the burden alone, he invited others to seek God with him, and God answered.

REFLECTION: When you find yourself in tough situations, who do you turn to? Do you have people who can pray for you? We are not meant to face life's challenges alone. In difficult moments, having faithful people who can pray with and for us strengthens our faith. When believers come together in agreement, God moves in powerful ways.

TODAY'S PRAYER: Father, thank You for the gift of prayer and community. Lead me to people who can faithfully pray for me, and help me to be someone others can rely on in times of need. Amen.

The Fiery Furnace

Read Daniel 3

SUMMARY: King Nebuchadnezzar had a gold statue built, and a decree was issued that whenever music was played, the people had to bow down to it. The decree also stated that those who refused to obey would be thrown into a fiery furnace.

Word got out that three Hebrew men, Shadrach, Meshach, and Abednego, had refused to bow down to the statue. Nebuchadnezzar had them thrown into the furnace, heated seven times hotter than usual. God protected them, and a fourth figure appeared in the fire with them. When the men came out unharmed, Nebuchadnezzar praised their God, acknowledged His power, and promoted Shadrach, Meshach, and Abednego.

REFLECTION: Following God does not always lead to immediate relief; sometimes it leads directly into difficulty. Yet faithfulness is proven not when obedience is easy, but when it is costly.

Shadrach, Meshach, and Abednego chose to honor God even when obedience meant facing the fire. They did not obey because they were guaranteed deliverance, but because God was worthy of their trust. In the same way, we are called to remain faithful even when obedience brings hardship, uncertainty, or loss. Trust that God is still at work in the fire, and that His presence is enough—no matter the outcome.

TODAY'S PRAYER: Father, give me the courage to obey You even when it is difficult or comes at a cost. Help me to remain faithful when obedience leads to hardship, trusting that Your presence is with me in every trial. Amen.

King Nebuchadnezzar is Humbled

Read Daniel 4:28-37

SUMMARY: One day, King Nebuchadnezzar proudly surveyed Babylon and claimed it was built by his own power for his glory. Immediately, a voice from heaven declared that his kingdom would be taken from him. Within the hour, Nebuchadnezzar was driven from society and lived among wild animals, eating grass like cattle, until his hair grew long and his nails resembled birds' claws. When the appointed time passed, he humbled himself, praised God, and his kingdom was restored with even greater honor.

REFLECTION: Nebuchadnezzar's story serves as a powerful reminder of how easily pride can take root when success is left unchecked. Always be mindful that it is not by our own strength or abilities that we have achieved any measure of success. Any skills or talents that we have are gifts from God to us. Just as easily as God can give a position, He can remove it. May we choose to walk in humility daily, so that God does not have to humble us.

TODAY'S PRAYER: Father, forgive me for the moments where I took credit for Your blessings. I acknowledge that nothing that I have done is by my own works or abilities. I pray that You will keep me in a posture of humility. Amen.

Handwriting on the Wall

Read Daniel 5

SUMMARY: King Belshazzar, the grandson of Nebuchadnezzar, held a feast for his nobles and used sacred cups taken from the temple in Jerusalem while praising idol gods. Suddenly, a hand appeared and wrote on the palace wall. None of the wise men could interpret the message, so Daniel was called. Daniel explained that the writing was God's judgment against Belshazzar for his pride and for dishonoring God, despite knowing how God had humbled his grandfather. That very night, Belshazzar was killed, and Daniel was promoted.

Belshazzar knew the lessons of the past but failed to apply them. Instead of humbling himself, he openly disrespected God, proving that knowledge without obedience leads to judgment.

REFLECTION: Belshazzar's story challenges us to learn from the mistakes of those who came before us. Are there patterns, habits, or struggles in your family history that need to end with you? God gives us opportunities to break generational cycles, but we must be willing to act. Go to therapy, take financial classes, break the addiction. Let the generational curse end with you. It won't be easy, but if you don't learn from the mistakes of the past, you'll have to face the "handwriting on the wall" in your own life.

TODAY'S PRAYER: Father, thank You for allowing me to learn through the experiences of others. Give me wisdom and discernment to recognize those lessons and the courage to break unhealthy patterns in my life. Amen.

Daniel in the Lion's Den

Read Daniel 6

SUMMARY: A few men did not like Daniel, so they convinced King Darius to issue a decree that individuals who worshiped or prayed to anyone besides the king would be thrown into the lion's den. Though Daniel knew the law, he continued to pray to God. King Darius was distressed but had no choice but to enforce the decree, sending Daniel into the lion's den. The next morning, Daniel was found unharmed, and the king witnessed the power of God.

The officials were jealous of Daniel. He was a foreigner, he didn't play by their rules, and yet he continued to be favored.

REFLECTION: Sometimes, people may be jealous of you for being favored by God. They may envy your calling or your talents. They may desire your level of influence. Let this story encourage you. Keep being you and keep walking in your calling. Continue to move forward and progress. Don't allow the negativity of others to sway you. God is your protector, and what is meant to harm you cannot succeed.

TODAY'S PRAYER: Father, thank You for Your protection and favor. Strengthen me to keep moving forward despite opposition, and guard my heart and mind from negativity. Amen.

Hosea

Read Hosea 1

SUMMARY: God told the prophet Hosea to marry Gomer, a woman described as an unfaithful prostitute, as a symbol of Israel's unfaithfulness to Him. Hosea and Gomer had three children, each with a meaningful name: Jezreel, symbolizing God's judgment on Israel; Lo-Ruhamah, meaning "no mercy," showing God's temporary withdrawal of compassion; and Lo-Ammi, meaning "not my people," representing Israel's broken relationship with God. Through Hosea's family, God illustrated the seriousness of sin, the consequences of turning from Him, and the hope of His eventual restoration.

Hosea's obedience required deep personal sacrifice and public humiliation. His life became a living representation of the cost of following God and trusting Him without reservation.

REFLECTION: At times, God may allow our lives to serve as lessons for others. In moments of hardship, people may be watching to see whether we will remain faithful or turn away. Even when we don't understand the purpose behind our suffering, we can trust that God is working through it. Our trials may not always end neatly, but maintaining faith and an eternal perspective gives us hope beyond our circumstances.

TODAY'S PRAYER: Father, even during my trials and tribulations, I acknowledge that You are good. Help me to find hope and peace in the midst of darkness. May the way that I handle my bad days be a reflection of Your goodness. Amen.

Jonah and the Big Fish

Read Jonah 1

SUMMARY: The Lord instructed Jonah to go to the city of Nineveh and preach against their sinful ways. Jonah, however, chose to board a ship that was going in the opposite direction to avoid the Lord's instructions. As a result, the Lord caused a big storm to come that threatened to destroy the ship. The men on board realized that Jonah was the reason for the terrible storm and threw him overboard. A big fish swallowed Jonah, and he remained inside the fish for three days and three nights.

REFLECTION: It's easy to judge Jonah for being disobedient, but we've all had moments where God told us to do something, and we disobeyed. Whether we disobeyed out of fear, laziness, or even doubt, we eventually had to face the consequences of our disobedience, surrender to God, and ask for forgiveness.

We have to remember that God is all-powerful. Regardless of the decisions we make, His will is going to be done. You can either surrender willingly or end up surrendering from the "belly" of your disobedience. Do yourself a favor today and choose the easier path.

TODAY'S PRAYER: Father, I acknowledge that I'm not always as obedient to You as I should be. I ask for Your forgiveness. Give me the strength to surrender to Your will, even if it's not what I want to do. Amen.

Jonah Prays

Read Jonah 2

SUMMARY: While inside the fish, Jonah prayed to the Lord. The Lord heard him and made the fish spit Jonah out onto the beach.

Some people may see Jonah being trapped inside the fish as a punishment for running away, but when reading Jonah 2, the unusual imprisonment turned out to be a blessing. The time alone gave Jonah a chance to reflect on his relationship with God. He was able to recall how God always heard him and protected him. Jonah had a change of heart while inside the fish. He went from attempting to run away from God to reaching out to God.

REFLECTION: Seasons of isolation can feel like punishment, but they may be opportunities for growth. God can use times of separation to draw us closer to Himself and realign our hearts. When God seeks our attention, He may remove distractions so we can focus on Him. If you find yourself feeling alone, use that time to seek God—He may be preparing you for what comes next or working within you.

TODAY'S PRAYER: Father, thank You that You are always there for me, even when I feel alone. Help me to use moments of isolation to seek Your face and learn about You. Make Your presence known, instruct me, and direct me. Amen.

Jonah Goes to Nineveh

Read Jonah 3

SUMMARY: The Lord instructed Jonah to go to Nineveh again, and this time he was obedient. When Jonah arrived and shared God's warning, the people of Nineveh were receptive. Everyone, including the king, went on a fast and wore burlap to demonstrate their humility and sorrow. When God saw their sincerity and how they had turned away from wickedness, He did not follow through with His threat of destruction.

The Bible says that the people of Nineveh were wicked, but the Lord still gave them forty days after Jonah's warning to get right. Their repentance was not only expressed outwardly but also demonstrated through changed actions. They prayed to God and stopped their evil ways. That was when God changed His mind and held back their punishment.

REFLECTION: When you commit a sin and ask for forgiveness, do you just feel bad, or do you intend to change? So often we can be repentant verbally, and we may even think that we mean it, but God is looking for more. He wants a heart change. God wants our actions to reflect our words. Let us be mindful that we all will sin and fall short, but when it happens, we need to show God that we mean what we say and turn away from unrighteousness.

TODAY'S PRAYER: Father, thank You for giving second chances. I don't want to take Your grace for granted. Help me to truly turn away from my sins and follow You. Amen.

Jonah is Angry with God

Read Jonah 4

SUMMARY: Jonah was angry when God chose to spare Nineveh, his enemies. He complained to the Lord, admitting that he knew God was gracious and merciful, and quick to forgive—which is why he didn't want to preach to the Ninevites in the first place. Jonah was so upset that he asked God to take his life.

God caused a plant to grow and provide Jonah with shade, bringing him comfort. But the next day, God sent a worm to destroy the plant, and Jonah became angry again. The Lord then used the plant to teach Jonah a lesson. If Jonah could care so deeply about a plant that he had no part in creating, how much more should God care about the people of Nineveh?

REFLECTION: Jonah's response challenges us to examine our own hearts. Do we limit who deserves to hear about God's grace? God's mercy is not reserved for those who look like us, think like us, or make us comfortable. He desires that all would repent and be saved. As believers, we are called to reflect God's love to everyone—without favoritism.

TODAY'S PRAYER: Father, thank You for loving everyone equally. Help me to reflect Your grace and be willing to share Your truth with everyone, even those I find difficult to love. Amen.

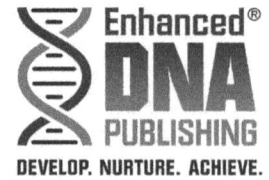

www.ingramcontent.com/pod-product-compliance
Lightning Source LLC
Chambersburg PA
CBHW070642160426
43194CB00009B/1551